# Echoes Of Divinity

Amanda Ventura

Published by Amanda Ventura, 2024.

While every precaution has been taken in the preparation of this book, the publisher assumes no responsibility for errors or omissions, or for damages resulting from the use of the information contained herein.

ECHOES OF DIVINITY

**First edition. September 6, 2024.**



ISBN: 979-8227637222

Written by Amanda Ventura.

Echoes Of Divinity
Amanda Ventura

# Dedication

I am deeply honored to dedicate this book to all the readers, with the heartfelt aspiration that its message will resonate far and wide, illuminating even the loneliest of places with a beacon of hope. Your unwavering support and engagement with the words within these pages hold immeasurable significance to me, and I am profoundly grateful for your presence on this journey. May the sentiments expressed within these chapters serve as a source of inspiration, solace, and upliftment regardless of where you find yourself along your path. Your participation in this shared experience is cherished beyond measure, and I hope that the essence of this book ignites within you a newfound sense of inner resilience, unyielding strength, and the courage needed to triumph over any obstacles that life may present. Your personal journey stands as a testament to the profound impact of perseverance and determination. Keep shining brightly, dear reader, for your resilience and unwavering spirit are a beacon of light for us all.

ACKNOWLEDGMENT

I would like to extend my heartfelt gratitude to my dear friend Tony (Inkwell Book Writer) and his team, for giving me the strength, courage, and unwavering support throughout the process of publishing this book. Your positive advice, encouragement, and the tireless efforts of your team have been invaluable. Thank you for believing in me and standing by my side every step of the way. Your friendship and support mean the world to me.

# CONTENTS

# Chapter One

INTRODUCTION

In a world often cloaked in darkness, there exist beings of pure light and compassion known as Earth Angels. These celestial beings walk among us, spreading their infectious positivity and unwavering love to all they encounter. Embarking upon new adventures with unyielding determination, Earth Angels face adversity, challenges, and obstacles head on, turning each trial into a stepping stone towards greater growth and understanding. As beacons of hope and inspiration, they serve as a reminder that even in the midst of chaos, light will always prevail. Join these Earth Angels on their journey as they navigate the complexities of life, shining brightly and illuminating the path for others to follow.

# Chapter One

In the quiet corners of the world, where the hum of civilization faded into a soft whisper, a group of beings stood poised between the realms of the divine and the mundane. These were not the ethereal figures of gilded art or the dramatic silhouettes of ancient texts, they were the Angels among us beings of light and purpose, cloaked in the guise of humanity. Their mission was not one of grandiosity or spectacle but a subtle weaving of hope and guidance into the fabric of everyday life.

The sun had barely risen over the small town of Eldason when the first of these angels arrived at the local diner, a modest establishment known as The Maple Loft. It was a place where the clinking of coffee cups and the sizzling of bacon created a symphony of morning rituals. As the door swung open, a gentle chime announced the arrival of a newcomer. Her name was Seraphina, and she appeared to be in her late twenties, with chestnut hair that cascaded in waves down her back and eyes that sparkled with an otherworldly light.

Seraphina took a seat at the counter, her presence instantly altering the atmosphere. Regulars, engrossed in their conversations, paused and glanced her way, drawn by an inexplicable sense of comfort that enveloped her. She ordered a simple breakfast a stack of pancakes drizzled with maple syrup and a side of fresh fruit. As she waited, she observed the people around her, her heart attuned to their unspoken struggles and dreams.

Eldason was a town marked by its charm, yet it was not without its shadows. The economic downturn had left many families struggling, and the weight of unfulfilled aspirations hung heavy in the air. Seraphina understood this; her purpose was to bring light to these shadows, to guide those who had lost their way. She had chosen this town for its potential, for the strength of its people, and for the stories that lay hidden beneath the surface.

As she savored her breakfast, Seraphina's attention was drawn to a young mother seated a few stools down. The woman, Emma, was juggling a toddler on her lap while trying to eat her own breakfast. Her face was etched with fatigue, and her eyes betrayed a deep-seated worry. Seraphina felt a pull toward her, an innate understanding that this was a moment meant for intervention.

Excuse me, Seraphina said, her voice warm and melodic, I couldn't help but notice how busy you are. Would you like me to hold your little one for a moment?

Emma looked up, surprise flickering across her features. Oh, that's very kind of you, but

Please, Seraphina insisted gently. I'd love to help.

With a hesitant smile, Emma handed her toddler over, and in that simple act, a connection was forged. Seraphina cradled the child, who giggled at her, oblivious to the weight of the world that pressed down on his mother. As Emma took a breath, the tension in her shoulders eased, and for the first time that morning, she allowed herself a moment of respite.

Thank you, Emma said, her voice thick with emotion. It's been a rough few weeks. My husband lost his job, and I'm trying to keep everything together.

Seraphina nodded, her heart swelling with empathy. Sometimes, we all need a little help. It's okay to lean on others.

Emma looked into Seraphina's eyes, and in that moment, she felt seen truly seen. It was as if Seraphina had peeled back the layers of her struggle and exposed the rawness of her vulnerability. They talked, and with every word exchanged, Seraphina offered not just comfort but also a sense of hope. She shared stories of resilience, of people who had faced adversity and emerged stronger, and Emma found herself inspired.

As the morning unfolded, more patrons entered The Maple Loft, each carrying their own burdens. There was Thomas, an elderly man who had recently lost his wife, Tamara, a high school student grappling with the pressures of impending exams, and Marcus, a mechanic who had dreams of becoming an artist but felt trapped in his current life. Seraphina moved among them, her presence a balm to their wounds. She listened, offered encouragement, and, in her subtle way, illuminated paths that had seemed obscured by darkness.

The diner buzzed with a newfound energy, laughter mingling with the aroma of freshly brewed coffee. Seraphina's influence was palpable; she had become a catalyst for connection, reminding each person of their worth and the strength that resided within them. By the time she finished her breakfast, the once somber atmosphere had transformed into one of camaraderie and hope.

As she prepared to leave, Emma approached her, gratitude shining in her eyes. You have a gift, Seraphina. You've brought light into our lives today.

Seraphina smiled, her heart swelling with joy.

We all have the capacity to bring light to one another. Sometimes, it just takes a little reminder.

With that, she stepped out into the crisp morning air, the sun now fully risen and casting a golden hue over Eldason. She felt the energy of the town shift, a ripple of newfound hope spreading among its inhabitants. But her work was far from over. There were more souls to touch, more shadows to illuminate.

As she walked down the street, she sensed the presence of her fellow angels, each engaged in their own missions, weaving through the lives of those who needed them most. They were teachers, healers, artists, and everyday heroes, each one a beacon of light in a world that often felt dim. Their purpose was to remind humanity of its inherent goodness, to inspire kindness, and to foster connections that transcended the barriers of fear and doubt.

Seraphina paused at the corner of Maple and Oak, taking a moment to breathe in the beauty of the day. The chirping of birds, the laughter of children playing, and the rustle of leaves in the gentle breeze all spoke of life's intricate tapestry. She knew that her journey had just begun, that each day would present new challenges and opportunities to uplift those around her.

With renewed determination, she set off to explore the heart of Eldason, ready to embrace whatever awaited her. For she was an angel among them, and her purpose was clear: to be a guiding light in the lives of those who had forgotten how to shine.

# Chapter Two

The sun hung high in the sky, casting its warm glow over the town of Eldason, but within Seraphina's heart, a chill began to creep in. Despite the laughter and warmth she had fostered at The Maple Loft, she felt an undercurrent of resistance swirling around her, a dissonance that threatened to overshadow the light she was trying to spread. It was a familiar sensation, one she had encountered before, yet it never ceased to unsettle her.

As she wandered through the streets, her senses heightened. She could feel the weight of unspoken fears and insecurities clinging to the townspeople like a heavy fog. It was as if the very act of bringing light into their lives had awakened something dark within them, an instinctive fear of the unknown, a reluctance to confront the shadows they carried. Seraphina understood this struggle intimately; she had been sent to Earth for a reason, to illuminate the paths of those who had lost their way, but she also knew that not everyone welcomed the light.

Her next stop was the local park, a serene oasis in the heart of Eldason. Children played on the swings, their laughter ringing like music through the air, while couples strolled hand in hand, basking in the beauty of the day. Yet, as Seraphina approached, she noticed a figure sitting alone on a bench, shrouded in a cloud of despondency. It was Marcus, the mechanic she had encountered earlier at the diner. His brow was furrowed, and his hands fidgeted restlessly in his lap.

Marcus, she called softly, approaching him with a warm smile. Mind if I join you? He looked up, surprise flickering in his eyes before he nodded. Sure, why not?

As she sat beside him, Seraphina could feel the heaviness that enveloped him, an aura of self doubt and frustration that seemed to cling to his very being. What's on your mind? she asked gently, her voice a soothing balm.

He sighed deeply, his shoulders slumping. It's just... I don't know if I can keep going like this. Every day feels the same. I wake up, go to work, and come home to an empty house. I've always wanted to be an artist, but I can't seem to find the courage to pursue it. I feel trapped."

Seraphina's heart ached for him. You have a gift, Marcus. I saw it in your eyes when you spoke about your passion. Why don't you believe in yourself?

He shook his head, frustration bubbling to the surface. Because every time I try to put myself out there, I hear the voices in my head telling me I'm not good enough. It's like a constant battle between what I want and what I think I can achieve. And it's exhausting.

In that moment, Seraphina understood the struggle all too well. She had faced her own demons whispers of inadequacy and fear that threatened to drown out her purpose. But she also knew that the light she carried within her had the power to silence those voices, if only for a moment.

Marcus, she said, her voice firm yet gentle, what if I told you that the only way to find your wings is to leap? You have to take that first step, even if it feels daunting. You won't know what you're capable of until you try.

He looked at her, uncertainty flickering in his eyes. But what if I fail? Failure is part of the journey, Seraphina replied, her heart swelling with conviction. Every artist, every dreamer has faced it. It's not about the destination, it's about the courage to pursue what sets your soul on fire. You have that fire within you, Marcus. Don't let it dim.

As she spoke, she could feel the shadows around him begin to shift, the darkness that had clung to his spirit slowly receding. It was a small victory, yet it felt monumental. But even as she encouraged him, Seraphina sensed the presence of something darker lurking just beyond the edges of her perception a resistance that seemed to pulse with energy, a silent protest against the light.

Suddenly, the atmosphere around them shifted. A group of teenagers, drawn by curiosity, approached the park bench. They were loud and boisterous, their laughter echoing through the air, but there was an edge to their demeanor a sense of entitlement that prickled at Seraphina's skin. One of them, a tall boy with a cocky grin, sauntered over, his eyes narrowing as he took in the scene.

What's this? A little heart to heart? He sneered, crossing his arms. You really think you're going to inspire him? Look at you, sitting here like some kind of fairy godmother.

Seraphina felt a surge of energy ripple through her, an instinctive urge to shield Marcus from the negativity radiating from the boy. But she also knew that engaging in a battle of words would only escalate the situation. Instead, she focused her gaze on Marcus, who had visibly tensed at the intrusion.

Marcus, she said softly, remember what I told you about the fire within you. Don't let anyone else's darkness extinguish it.

The boy scoffed, rolling his eyes. What a joke. You really think you can change anything? People like you don't belong here.

Seraphina felt the weight of his words, a reminder of the resistance she often faced when trying to bring light into the world. It was a struggle she had encountered time and again people who were threatened by the light, who clung to their shadows out of fear or ignorance. But she refused to let his words pierce her resolve.

"Everyone deserves a chance to shine, she replied, her voice steady. Even those who may not understand it yet.

The boy laughed, a harsh sound that cut through the air. You think you're some kind of angel, don't you? Well, newsflash! not everyone wants your help.

With that, he turned on his heel, strutting away with his friends, leaving a trail of laughter that felt like a taunt. Seraphina's heart sank, the weight of his words settling heavily on her shoulders. She glanced at Marcus, who looked as though he had shrunk in on himself, the spark she had ignited now dimmed.

Don't listen to them, she urged, but she could see the doubt creeping back into his eyes. You have the power to choose your own path.

I don't know if I can, he murmured, his voice barely above a whisper.

Seraphina reached out, placing a comforting hand on his arm. You can, and you will. It's okay to feel afraid. Just don't let that fear dictate your life. Remember, you are not alone in this.

As they sat in silence, a heavy stillness enveloping them, Seraphina felt the shadows closing in, their presence palpable and suffocating. It was a reminder that her work was not just about uplifting individuals, it was about confronting the darkness that lingered in the hearts of many. It was a battle against the very essence of fear and doubt that sought to extinguish the light.

With a deep breath, she resolved to continue her fight. The light she carried was not just for herself, it was for everyone who felt lost in the shadows. She would not shy away from the challenges ahead, nor would she allow the demons of others to dim her purpose.

As she stood to leave, she turned to Marcus, determination etched across her face. I believe in you, Marcus. Don't let anyone tell you otherwise. The world needs your art, your voice. Promise me you'll take that leap.

He looked up at her, uncertainty still lingering, but there was a flicker of something else, hope. I promise, he said, his voice stronger than before.

With that, Seraphina walked away from the park, her heart heavy but resolute. She could feel the shadows trailing behind her, but she refused to let them define her journey. She was an angel among them, and her purpose was clear, to shine brightly, even in the face of darkness, and to guide others toward their own light. The struggle would be ongoing but she was ready to embrace it one soul at a time.

# Chapter Three

In the town of Eldason, nestled among the rolling hills and whispering trees, Seraphina, an earth angel with a heart as vast as the sky above. She possessed a rare gift of healing and a gentle spirit that touched the souls of all who crossed her path. Despite her extraordinary abilities, Seraphina often found herself feeling isolated and alone in the bustling town.

The townspeople, though grateful for her presence and the miracles she performed, could not truly understand the weight of her divine responsibilities. Seraphina carried the burdens of others on her shoulders, absorbing their pain and suffering to bring them peace. But in doing so, she distanced herself from forming deep connections with anyone, for fear of burdening them with her own struggles.

As days turned into nights and seasons changed, Seraphina wandered the cobblestone streets of Eldason, her ethereal presence a beacon of light in the darkness. Yet, despite the admiration and respect she received, a deep sense of emptiness gnawed at her soul. She longed for someone to see beyond the facade of the earth angel, to understand the depths of her loneliness and offer solace in return.

One fateful evening, as the moon hung low in the sky and the stars shimmered like diamonds, Seraphina found herself drawn to the edge of town, where the whispers of the wind beckoned her to a secluded meadow. There, under the watchful gaze of the ancient oak tree, she collapsed to her knees, tears streaming down her face like silver rivers.

I am so tired of carrying the weight of the world on my shoulders, she whispered to the night, her voice trembling with raw emotion. I long for connection, for understanding, for a kindred spirit to share my burden.

To her surprise, a soft voice replied from the shadows, You are not alone, Seraphina. I have watched over you, unseen but ever present, drawn to your light in the darkness.

And from the shadows emerged a figure bathed in moonlight, their eyes reflecting the sorrow and longing that mirrored Seraphina's own. It was Lysander, a lost soul searching for meaning and belonging, whose heart resonated with the earth angel's silent plea for companionship.

In that moment, Seraphina and Lysander found solace in each other's presence, their souls intertwining like vines on a trellis. Together, they shared their fears, their dreams, and their deepest truths, finding in each other a kindred spirit that eased the ache of loneliness.

As the first light of dawn painted the sky in hues of rose and gold, Seraphina and Lysander stood hand in hand, their hearts entwined in a bond that transcended time and space. In each other, they had found the missing piece of their souls, a connection that would sustain them through the trials and tribulations that lay ahead.

And as they walked through the town of Eldason, their footsteps echoing in harmony, Seraphina knew that she was no longer alone. For in Lysander's eyes, she saw the reflection of her own light, shining bright and steadfast in the darkness. And in that shared light, they found the strength to face whatever challenges the future may hold, together, as kindred spirits bound by a love that defied all odds.

# Chapter Four

Seraphina had always felt like an outsider in the town of Eldason. The people there were polite enough, but there was a certain distance, a subtle coldness that kept her from truly feeling at home. That is, until she met Lysander.

From the moment they first crossed paths in the bustling marketplace, Seraphina felt a spark of connection with Lysander. He was unlike anyone she had ever met, kind, thoughtful, and with a deep well of sadness in his eyes that seemed to mirror her own. As they spent more time together, Seraphina found herself opening up to Lysander in a way she never had with anyone else. He became her confidant, her rock, the one person she could turn to when the weight of loneliness became too much to bear.

With Lysander by her side, Seraphina no longer felt alone in Eldason. His presence brought light to her days and warmth to her nights. They would roam the cobblestone streets together, sharing stories and dreams, finding solace in each other's company. But beneath the surface of their newfound happiness, a shadow loomed a shadow that whispered of uncertainty and fate's cruel hand.

As the days turned into weeks and the weeks into months, Seraphina couldn't shake the feeling of impending doom that hung over her and Lysander. It was as if the universe was conspiring to tear them apart, to test the strength of their bond. And then, one fateful night, tragedy struck.

A fire tore through Eldason, consuming everything in its path. Seraphina and Lysander found themselves trapped in the inferno, fighting for their lives amidst the chaos and destruction. In those harrowing moments, as flames licked at their heels and smoke filled their lungs, Seraphina realized the depth of her feelings for Lysander. She couldn't bear the thought of losing him, of being alone once more in a world that had already taken so much from her.

But fate was unkind that night, and as the fire raged on, Seraphina and Lysander were torn apart. In the aftermath of the devastation, Seraphina searched desperately for any sign of her beloved companion, praying to the heavens for his safety. But her cries went unanswered, and all that remained was a gaping void where Lysander had once stood.

The flames roared like a beast unleashed, their heat engulfing everything in Eldason, a once vibrant town now turned into a hellish landscape. Seraphina and Lysander, though terrified, fought against the encroaching inferno, their hearts pounding in rhythm with the crackling fire. The smoke stung their eyes and filled their lungs, but in that moment of desperation, Seraphina felt an awakening within her, a realization that transcended the chaos surrounding them. It was a fierce, undeniable love for Lysander, a bond forged in laughter and shared dreams, now threatened by the very flames that sought to consume them. With each step they took, her determination to protect him grew, igniting a fire within her that rivaled the one outside.

As they navigated through the smoke filled streets, Seraphina's heart raced not just from the fear of the flames but from the overwhelming surge of emotions she had kept buried. Every glance at Lysander, his face set with resolve, made her heart ache with the thought of losing him. Memories of their shared moments laughter under the stars, whispered secrets in the quiet of the night flooded her mind, each one a reminder of what was at stake. She wanted to tell him, to confess the depth of her feelings, but the chaos around them drowned out her words. Instead, she clung to him, a silent promise that she would fight alongside him, no matter the odds.

But fate, as it often does, had other plans. In the midst of the turmoil, the ground beneath them trembled, and a sudden explosion sent debris crashing down, separating the two in an instant. Seraphina felt a gut wrenching panic as she turned, reaching for Lysander, but he was gone swallowed by the smoke and chaos. The world around her spiraled into a blur of flames and screams, and she was left standing alone, her heart shattering under the weight of despair. The fire raged on, but all she could see was the gaping void where Lysander had once stood, a cruel reminder of the fragility of life and love.

In the aftermath of the devastation, as dawn broke over the smoldering ruins of Eldason, Seraphina wandered through the ashes, her heart heavy with sorrow. The vibrant town she had known, the laughter they had shared, and the dreams they had nurtured were now nothing but memories, lost in the smoke. She called out for Lysander, her voice hoarse from tears and smoke, praying that somehow he had escaped the inferno. Each unanswered cry felt like a dagger to her heart, a reminder of the loneliness that threatened to consume her as thoroughly as the flames had consumed their home.

Desperation clawed at her as she searched through the wreckage, each step a painful reminder of what she had lost. The world felt cold and empty without Lysander by her side, and the thought of never seeing him again was a darkness she could hardly bear. Yet, amidst the ashes, a flicker of hope remained. Seraphina clung to the belief that love transcends even the most harrowing of circumstances. With every ounce of strength, she vowed to find him, to uncover the truth of what had happened, and to fight against the despair that threatened to engulf her. For in that moment of loss, she realized that her love for Lysander was not extinguished but rather a flame that would guide her through the darkest of nights.

Alone once more, Seraphina was left to mourn the loss of the one person who had made her feel truly alive in Eldason. The town that had once felt like a prison now seemed vast and empty, a cruel reminder of all that she had lost. And as she wandered the streets, her heart heavy with grief, Seraphina couldn't help but wonder what was to become of her now, in a world where even the brightest lights could be extinguished in an instant?

# Chapter Five

Seraphina's heart ached with a relentless sorrow that seemed to consume her very being. After losing Lysander, the one soul who had managed to touch the deepest parts of her own, she felt adrift in a world that no longer held any comfort. The memory of his absence haunted her every step, a constant reminder of the fragility of the connections she so desperately sought.

As an earth angel, Seraphina's purpose was to spread love and light to those around her. But with each passing day, she found it harder to muster the strength to fulfill her duty. The pain of losing Lysander had left a void in her heart that no amount of kindness could fill. It seemed that every time she let someone in, they would vanish from her life just as quickly, leaving her alone once more.

As Seraphina walked the cobblestone streets of Eldason, her heart a delicate tapestry of hope and despair. With every step, her heavy wings brushed against the ground, a constant reminder of the emotional weight she carried. Each feather, once vibrant and full of life, seemed dulled by the sorrow that enveloped her. She had once believed that love was a sanctuary, a place where her soul could find solace. But with each heartbreak, that sanctuary had crumbled, leaving her lost in a labyrinth of loneliness.

The sun dipped below the horizon, casting a golden hue that danced upon the rooftops, yet Seraphina felt none of its warmth. She paused outside of Maple Loft, its windows aglow with laughter and light, the air filled with the aroma of freshly brewed coffee and pastries. Inside, couples leaned into one another, their hands entwined, eyes shimmering with the promise of forever. The sight pierced her heart, a bittersweet reminder of what she longed for and feared to lose.

Just one touch, she whispered to herself, envisioning the embrace of a love that would cradle her insecurities and mend her fractured spirit. But the shadows of her past loomed large, whispering tales of abandonment. Each time she had dared to open her heart, she had been met with loss, each farewell a dagger that deepened the fissures within her soul.

Determined to shield herself from further heartache, Seraphina turned away from the Maple Loft, her wings folding tightly against her back, as if to protect her from the world that seemed so intent on breaking her. Yet, as she wandered through the quiet streets, she felt a flicker of something an ember of yearning that refused to be extinguished. The loneliness echoed in her chest, a haunting lullaby that called for connection.

Days melted into weeks, and Seraphina found herself drawn to a secluded garden at the edge of the city. It was a sanctuary of sorts, where the scent of blooming jasmine mingled with the soft rustling of leaves. Here, she would sit for hours, sketching the beauty around her, pouring her heart into the pages of her journal, hoping to capture the essence of happiness she so desperately craved.

One fateful evening, as the sky ignited in shades of lavender and gold, a figure entered the garden. He was a stranger, with eyes that sparkled like the stars above, and an easy smile that seemed to light up the twilight. Their gazes met, and in that moment, something stirred within Seraphina a flicker of hope, a whisper of possibility.

Are you an artist? he asked, glancing at her sketches scattered on the bench. His voice was warm, like a gentle breeze that brushed against her skin, awakening her senses.

I try, she replied, her heart racing. But it never feels quite enough. He stepped closer, studying her work with genuine curiosity. Art is about expression, not perfection. It's about capturing what you feel, and you have a gift.

As the days turned into weeks, Seraphina found herself drawn to him, his presence a balm to her wounded spirit. They shared stories, laughter, and moments of silence that spoke volumes. He saw her the entirety of her being, the light and the shadows and for the first time, she felt the weight of her heart lift, if only slightly.

Yet the specter of her past loomed large. Each time he reached for her hand or leaned in for a closer conversation, a flicker of doubt ignited in her chest. What if she lost him? What if this was just another chapter in a book of heartache? But with each passing day, she found the courage to let go of the chains that bound her to her fear.

One evening, as they sat beneath a canopy of stars, he turned to her, his expression earnest. Seraphina, you don't have to carry the weight of your past alone. I am here, and I choose to see you for all that you are. Let me be the one to hold you, to love you despite the risk.

Tears brimmed in her eyes as she felt the walls around her heart begin to crumble. In that moment, she realized that love was not just about the promise of forever, but about allowing oneself to be vulnerable, to embrace the uncertainty of connection.

With a deep breath, she reached out, intertwining her fingers with his. I want to try, she whispered, her voice a fragile promise. And as he enveloped her in his arms, Seraphina felt the warmth of companionship wrap around her like a soft embrace a light piercing through the darkness of her solitude.

In that moment, she understood that love, while fraught with risks, could also be a source of strength. Though the road ahead may be uncertain, she was ready to take flight once more, her heart open to the possibilities that lay ahead. With her wings unfurling, Seraphina chose to embrace the beauty of connection, daring to hope that perhaps, this time, love would hold her tightly, refusing to let go.

Despite her best efforts to shield herself from further heartache, Seraphina couldn't help but crave the warmth of companionship. She longed to be held in arms that promised to never let go, to be seen and loved for all that she was. But the fear of losing yet another piece of her shattered heart kept her trapped in a cycle of loneliness and despair.

And so, Seraphina wandered through the world with a heavy heart, her wings weighed down by the burden of her unending grief. She yearned for a love that would defy the cruel whims of fate, a love that would endure even in the darkest of times. But as the days turned into nights and the stars whispered their silent laments, she knew that such a love may forever remain out of reach.

In her quiet moments of solitude, Seraphina clung to the memories of Lysander, the one who had shown her a glimpse of what true love could be. And though his absence left a void that seemed insurmountable, she held onto the hope that one day, she would find the kind of love she so freely gave to others. Until then, she would continue to navigate the world with a heavy heart, aching for a love that may never come.

# Chapter Six

Seraphina, heart heavy with the weight of grief, made the difficult decision to leave the familiar streets of Eldason behind. The memories of losing Lysander lingered like a shadow, casting a pall over every corner of the town she once called home. With resolve in her eyes, she knew she needed a fresh start, a new beginning to heal the wounds of her shattered heart.

Seraphina stood in her small bedroom, the sunlight filtering through the sheer curtains, casting gentle patterns on the floor. The sight felt both familiar and foreign, a bittersweet reminder of the life she once cherished. Each piece of furniture, each trinket, echoed with laughter and warmth, but the laughter had faded, replaced by the heavy silence of loss. Lysander's absence weighed on her like a shroud, and she knew she could no longer remain in Eldason, a place that had become a gallery of her grief.

With careful deliberation, she opened her worn leather suitcase, its surface scratched and scuffed from years of use. Seraphina had held onto it since her college days, a relic of adventures past. Now, it served as a vessel for her hopes of renewal. She meticulously folded her clothes, the scent of lavender lingering from the sachet she had tucked inside. Each piece represented a part of her old life that she was ready to leave behind, even if it was difficult to admit.

As she packed, memories of Lysander surged like waves his laughter, the way his eyes sparkled with mischief, the comfort of his presence. They had shared dreams of travel, of exploring the world hand in hand, but now those dreams felt like a cruel joke. The weight of grief made her chest ache, but she also felt a flicker of determination. She would honor his memory by living fully, by seeking the joy they had once envisioned together.

With her suitcase finally closed, Seraphina stood at the threshold of her home, the door creaking softly as it swung open. She inhaled deeply, the air tinged with the scent of blooming jasmine from the garden. The town of Eldason held too many memories, each one a reminder of what she had lost. But today, she chose to step away from the shadows that haunted her.

The road ahead was wide and uncertain. She had considered her options carefully. The bustling streets of a distant city, full of life and energy, called to her like a siren. Could she find distraction there, burying her sadness in the crowds? Or would the quiet solitude of a remote countryside retreat provide the solace she desperately sought?

In the end, it was the whispers of nature that beckoned her. She decided on a small town, a place where she could breathe deeply and let the healing process begin. The thought of rolling hills, the sound of a gentle stream, and the rustle of leaves in the breeze filled her with a sense of peace she hadn't felt in years.

As she drove away from Eldason, the landscape transformed the flat, familiar streets giving way to rolling hills and open skies. The weight on her heart began to lift, replaced by a budding sense of possibility. Each mile brought her closer to a place where she could redefine herself, a canvas waiting for new colors.

Arriving at the town, Seraphina felt a sense of calm wash over her. The air was crisp and refreshing, infused with the scent of pine and wildflowers. She found a quaint home that overlooked a shimmering lake, its surface reflecting the vibrant hues of the setting sun. This would be her sanctuary, a place to mend her spirit and embrace the unknown.

In the following days, she immersed herself in the beauty around her long walks through the woods, moments of stillness by the lake, and evenings filled with the soft glow of candlelight as she explored her thoughts in a journal. With each passing day, Seraphina felt the shadows of her grief begin to dissipate, replaced by a growing sense of hope.

The journey to healing was not linear, but she learned to embrace the ebb and flow of her emotions. She found solace in the small things, the laughter of children playing by the water, the warmth of a friendly smile from a neighbor, and the comfort of a cup of tea on her porch as the stars began to twinkle overhead.

Seraphina's heart, once heavy with loss, began to open again. She realized that while Lysander would always be a part of her, she could carry his memory forward without being anchored by it. The world was vast and full of possibilities, and she was ready to explore.

With each new dawn, she took a step forward, writing her own story of resilience and renewal. In the embrace of her new home, Seraphina discovered that the path to healing was illuminated not only by the memories of the past but also by the promise of new beginnings.

The world lay open before her, with a heavy heart and a determined spirit, Seraphina set off on her journey into the unknown. The road stretched out before her like a ribbon of promise, leading her towards a future yet unwritten. As time passed beneath her feet, she found herself filled with a sense of liberation, a newfound freedom in leaving behind the pain of the past.

Wherever Seraphina's path may lead, one thing was certain she was no longer bound by the chains of sorrow that had held her captive in Eldason. With each step she took, she moved further away from the echoes of loss and closer towards a brighter tomorrow, guided by the light of hope that shone within her soul.

# Chapter Seven

Seraphina had just settled into her new home in the quaint town of Lottersville when a sudden and unexpected knock jolted her from her quiet evening routine. Curious and slightly apprehensive, she approached the door cautiously, only to find a familiar face staring back at her through the dimly lit evening.

It was a long lost friend of Lysander, her dear friend who had mysteriously disappeared without a trace. The visitor had heard whispers of Lysander's possible whereabouts and had followed a trail that led him to Seraphina's doorstep. With a mixture of relief and sadness, Seraphina invited the stranger into her home, eager to hear news of her missing friend.

As they settled into the cozy living room, the visitor hesitantly revealed the grim truth. Lysander had met a tragic end in a devastating fire that had ravaged the town of Eldason, leaving behind a trail of destruction and loss. Seraphina's heart sank at the news, the weight of grief heavy on her shoulders as she grappled with the reality of her friend's untimely demise.

The sun had long set over the small town of Eldason, casting a veil of darkness that felt heavier than the night itself. Inside a quaint living room, dimly lit by a flickering candle, Seraphina sat on a plush sofa, her fingers nervously tracing the patterns of the fabric. The air was thick with unspoken words, and the atmosphere was charged with an anticipation that made her heart race.

The visitor, a childhood friend named Shawna shifted in her seat, her expression a mix of trepidation and sorrow. After what felt like an eternity, she took a deep breath, her voice barely above a whisper, It's about Lysander,

Seraphina's pulse quickened, and an unsettling sense of dread washed over her. What happened? she asked, knowing deep down that the answer would change everything.

Shawna's eyes glistened with unshed tears as she revealed the grim truth. He didn't make it. There was a fire, a terrible fire that swept through Eldason. It took everything homes, memories and Lysander.

The words pierced through the cocoon of comfort the living room had once provided, leaving Seraphina reeling. The weight of grief settled heavily upon her, an anchor that threatened to pull her under. She felt as if the very ground beneath her had crumbled away, leaving her adrift in a sea of loss.

The silence that followed was palpable, a heavy blanket that enveloped them both. In that stillness, memories of better times came rushing back laughter echoing in sunlit parks, late night adventures filled with dreams and secrets, and the warmth of friendship that had always been a constant in her life. Each recollection brought with it a bittersweet pang, a reminder of what was lost and what could never be regained.

Shawna, sensing Seraphina's turmoil, reached out, her hand resting gently on her friend's. I know this hurts, but we're in this together, she reassured, her voice steady despite the quiver of emotion. We've always been there for each other, and now... now is no different.

As the night deepened around them, the candle flickering in the dim light, the two friends found solace in each other's company. They shared stories of Lysander, painting vivid pictures of his laughter and kindness, allowing the warmth of their memories to stave off the encroaching darkness of grief. With every shared memory, they forged a bond that felt unbreakable, a testament to the power of friendship in the face of heartache.

Hours melted away as they reminisced, their laughter mingling with tears a beautiful symphony of sorrow and joy. In that cozy living room, beneath the weight of their shared grief, they discovered a flicker of hope. They realized that though Lysander was gone, his spirit lived on in their hearts, and the love they had shared would forever bind them together.

As dawn began to break, casting a soft glow through the curtains, Seraphina felt a sense of peace settling within her. The road ahead would be long and fraught with challenges, but with Shawna by her side, she knew she would not have to walk it alone. Together, they would honor Lysander's memory and carry the light of their friendship forward, illuminating the shadows of loss with the warmth of love and remembrance.

In the somber silence that followed, memories of better times flooded back, bringing both solace and sorrow to the two friends. And as the night grew darker around them, they found comfort in each other's company, united in their shared grief and the bond of friendship that transcended time and distance.

Despite the shadows of loss that lingered in the air, Seraphina and her unexpected visitor found solace in each other's presence, a beacon of light in the darkness of uncertainty. And as the night wore on, they shared stories of Lysander, keeping his memory alive in their hearts and minds, finding a sense of closure and connection in the midst of tragedy.

# Chapter Eight

In the tranquil town of Lottersville, the evening descended with a gentle grace. Seraphina bid Lysander friend farewell and set out into the fading light, leaving Seraphina to retire to the solace of her humble abode.

Exhausted from the day's endeavors, she sought refuge in the embrace of her soft bed, her mind drifting into a peaceful slumber as the whispers of the night enveloped her.

The quietude of the town wrapped around her like a warm blanket, cradling her in its serene embrace. And as the night deepened, Lottersville held its secrets close, guarding them with a silent watchfulness that seemed to echo in the stillness of the night.

As Seraphina lay in her narrow bed, her mind abuzz with the events of the day. Living in Lottersville nestled in the heart of the town. It was a quiet town, one that Seraphina cherished due to her being an earth angel who is always sensitive to her environment and all energies surrounding her. But lately, she couldn't shake the feelings that something was missing.

As she closed her eyes and drifted off to sleep, she felt a soft whisper in her ear. At first, she thought it was just a dream, a product of her overactive imagination. But the voice was insistent, and she found herself unable to ignore it.

Seraphina, the voice said, I have a task for you. A light that needs to be spread throughout the world. Will you help me?

Seraphina's heart raced as she sat up in bed, her eyes wide open. She looked around the room, but she was alone. The voice had disappeared as suddenly as it appeared.

But the voice was insistent, and she found herself unable to ignore it. Seraphina, the voice said, I have a task for you. A light that needs to be spread throughout the world. Will you help me?

Seraphina's heart raced as she sat up in bed, her eyes wide open. She looked around the room, but she was alone. The voice had disappeared as suddenly as it appeared, leaving her in an eerie silence. Confusion wrapped around her like a shroud, she had always been the practical sort, dismissing tales of whispers in the dark as mere fantasies for children.

Yet, as she lay back down, the whisper echoed in her mind. A light that needs to be spread. The phrase lingered, a haunting melody that pulled at her heartstrings. What could it mean? Who was speaking to her, and why her?

Days turned into weeks, and the memory of the voice faded into the background of her busy life. Seraphina was a dedicated seamstress tirelessly caring for others. She was known for her gentle touch and comforting presence, bringing hope to those who had lost it. But inside, she felt a growing emptiness, a restlessness that gnawed at her soul.

One evening, as she sat in her dimly lit home, the whisper returned, weaving through her thoughts like a thread of silver in the night. Seraphina, the light, it urged again, more fervent this time. You must seek it out.

With a sigh, she abandoned her exhaustion and picked up her notebook, the one she used to jot down ideas and dreams. She began to write, pouring her heart onto the pages. What if the light is kindness? she pondered, What if it's the laughter of children or the beauty of a sunset?Each word ignited a flicker of understanding within her, a dawning realization that the light she sought was embedded in the very fabric of human connection.

The next day, Seraphina made a decision. She would embark on a journey, not to find the light but to share it. She reached out to her community, organizing small acts of kindness a food drive for the homeless, a visit to the local nursing home, and a storytelling night for children at the library. Each event was like a brushstroke on a canvas, painting moments of joy and compassion in the lives of others.

As weeks passed, Seraphina's heart began to heal. The laughter of children echoed in her ears, the smiles of grateful strangers warmed her soul, and she discovered a profound truth, the light wasn't something to be found, it was something to be created, nurtured, and shared.

But just when she felt the warmth of fulfillment, the darkness crept back in. One chilly evening, she received a call that shattered her newfound peace. A young boy named Josh, whom she had grown fond of during his long battle with illness, had taken a turn for the worse. He had been her beacon of hope, a testament to resilience, and now he was slipping away.

Seraphina rushed to the hospital, her heart heavy with dread. She found Josh in his room, frail and pale, surrounded by the sterile white of hospital walls that felt more like a prison than a sanctuary. She sat by his bedside, holding his small hand in her own, whispering words of comfort. You're so strong, Josh. You can do this. You're my little warrior, she said, fighting back tears.

But as the night wore on, she could see the light fading from his eyes. The monitors beeped with a rhythm that felt like a cruel countdown to an inevitable end. In those moments, Seraphina remembered the voice, the insistent plea to spread the light. But how could she do that when darkness loomed so close?

Josh's mother entered the room, her face a mask of despair. Seraphina could see the weight of fear in her eyes, a reflection of her own. They exchanged a silent understanding, two souls bound by grief, but something flickered in Seraphina's heart. In that moment, she realized that even in the face of despair, there was a light to be found in love and presence.

Josh, she said softly, can you hear me? He opened his eyes, a faint glimmer of recognition passing through his gaze.

Seraphina? he whispered, his voice barely a breath.

Yes, it's me, she replied, squeezing his hand gently. You're not alone. We're all here for you.

With a flicker of a smile, Josh's eyes brightened for a moment. In that precious instant, Seraphina understood that the light she had been searching for wasn't just about acts of kindness, it was about the connection between people, the love that transcended even the darkest moments.

As the hours passed, Josh slipped away, his small hand growing cold in hers. But even in that sorrow, Seraphina felt a shift within herself. She had shared light with him in his final moments, and she knew that in her heart, he would always remain a part of her.

After the funeral, Seraphina found herself standing in front of the hospital, the weight of loss heavy on her shoulders. But she remembered the laughter of children, the warmth of shared stories, and the glimmers of connection she had cultivated in her community. She realized that Josh's light would live on through her, through the kindness she spread and the love she shared.

With renewed purpose, she returned to her mission, more determined than ever. She began to create workshops for families dealing with grief, offering a space for healing and understanding. She organized events that celebrated life and love, reminding all who attended that even in darkness, there was always the potential for light.

And as she lay down each night, the whisper returned, but it was different now. Seraphina, it would say, you have spread the light. You have fulfilled your task.

And in those moments, she smiled, knowing she was never truly alone. The whispers were no longer just a figment of her imagination, they were the echoes of love and connection that she had nurtured, a reminder that even the saddest stories could give birth to the most beautiful lights.

But the words lingered in her mind, but she couldn't shake the feeling that they were meant for her. She had always felt a sense of purpose, a calling to do something greater than herself. Could this be it?

# Chapter Nine

Seraphina woke up the next day with a sense of purpose. She remembered her dream vividly, and the voice that had spoken to her in the night. She knew she had to take action to follow the path set out before her.

She got dressed and packed a small bag with some food and supplies. She didn't know what she would find in Lottersville but she wanted to be prepared for anything.

The journey to Lottersville was a long one, but she didn't mind. She enjoyed the fresh air and the feeling of the sun on her face. She passed through fields of wildflowers and thick forests, marveling at the beauty of the world around her.

When she finally arrived to Lottersville, she was struck by how different the towns homes differed from hers. The houses were larger and grander, and there were people everywhere, bustling about.

She had dressed deliberately that morning, opting for her favorite faded blue dress, the one that danced around her knees with every step. After packing a small bag with essentials a few sandwiches, a bottle of water, and a worn out journal she took a deep breath, feeling a mixture of excitement and trepidation. She didn't know what she would find in Lottersville, but she wanted to be prepared for anything.

The journey stretched before her like a ribbon of hope. With every step, she was buoyed by the thrill of adventure, her heart racing at the thought of what lay ahead. The fresh air filled her lungs, invigorating her spirit, while the sun cast warm rays upon her skin, a gentle reminder that the world was alive and that she, too, was a part of it. She wandered through fields of wildflowers swaying in the breeze, their vibrant colors painting the landscape with joy. Thick forests loomed nearby, their tall trees whispering secrets in the wind, drawing her further into the embrace of nature.

As she walked, her mind danced with dreams of new beginnings. She envisioned Lottersville as a place where she could shed the weight of her past, a small town where laughter echoed through the streets, where strangers became friends over shared stories and warm smiles.

But as her journey continued, the landscape began to shift. The sun dipped lower in the sky, casting long shadows that twisted and turned like the uncertainty in her heart. She had heard whispers of Lottersville from travelers who had passed through the small town, tales of its beauty and charm, but she could not shake the feeling that something was amiss.

When she finally arrived in Lottersville, the sight before her was breathtaking yet daunting. The houses were larger and grander than anything she had ever seen, their ornate facades standing proudly against the backdrop of a vibrant sky. People bustled about, their faces a blur of purpose and urgency, lost in their own worlds. Instead of the warmth she had anticipated, she felt an overwhelming sense of isolation, as though she were a ghost drifting through a realm of the living.

As she wandered the streets, she tried to engage with the townsfolk, her heart yearning for connection. She approached a group of women chatting animatedly by a market stall, but they barely acknowledged her presence, their laughter ringing hollow in her ears. A young boy playing with a wooden toy glanced up at her, his eyes wide with curiosity, but his mother quickly pulled him away, casting her a wary look.

The vibrant life around her felt like a wall, separating her from the warmth of human connection. She took a seat on a bench, pulling her knees to her chest, the weight of loneliness settling upon her like a heavy cloak. She opened her journal, the pages blank and waiting, but the words she longed to write felt trapped inside her, suffocated by the fear of rejection.

As the day wore on, the sun began to set, casting a golden hue over the town. The beauty of the light was bittersweet, and she couldn't help but feel a pang of longing for the comfort of familiarity. The laughter and chatter continued around her, but it felt like a distant melody, one that she could never quite grasp.

Determined to make the most of her journey, she decided to explore further. She wandered down a narrow street, where the houses stood shoulder to shoulder, their windows glowing like fireflies in the dusk. She paused in front of a small bookstore, its wooden sign creaking in the breeze. The scent of old paper wafted through the door, inviting her in.

Inside, the warmth of the shop enveloped her, and for a moment, she felt a flicker of hope. She browsed the shelves, running her fingers along the spines of countless stories, each one a doorway to a different world. She picked up a book and sank into a chair, losing herself in its pages.

But as the minutes turned to hours, the reality of her solitude crept back in. The shopkeeper, a kind elderly woman, offered her a cup of tea, but even that small gesture couldn't fill the void within her. She smiled politely, thanked her, but felt the emptiness deepening.

The stars began to twinkle outside, a million tiny lights against the darkening sky. She knew it was time to leave, but as she stepped back into the cool night air, the weight of her disappointment pressed heavily on her chest. Lottersville had not been the sanctuary she had hoped for, instead, it felt like a mirage, beautiful yet ultimately unwelcoming.

As she made her way through the quiet streets, she reflected on what she had expected from this journey. She had sought connection, community, and a sense of belonging. But instead, she found herself more alone than ever, an outsider in a town that seemed to thrive on its own rhythm.

With each step, the realization settled in that perhaps she would never truly belong in Lottersville. She sat on a stone wall at the edge of the town, watching as the last remnants of light faded into the horizon. The beauty of the world around her was still there, but it felt as if it had dimmed just a little, overshadowed by the weight of her heartache.

She pulled out her journal once more, the pages blank and waiting as her tears fell onto the paper, smudging the emptiness with the ink of her sorrow. She wrote about her journey, the wildflowers, the laughter of the townsfolk, and the ache of loneliness that wrapped around her like a shroud.

As the night deepened, she realized that her journey to Lottersville might have been more than a quest for connection, it was also an exploration of her own heart. And though she felt lost and alone, she understood that every step she took, every tear she shed, was a part of her story a story that was still being written, filled with both heartache and hope.

With a heavy heart but a flicker of resilience, she closed her journal and stood up. She would return home, but this experience would remain etched in her soul, a reminder that even in the depths of loneliness, the journey itself held the power to transform and heal.

She took a deep breath, the cool night air filling her lungs. Moving forward, she resolved to carry the lessons of Lottersville with her, ready to face whatever came next, knowing that she was more than just a solitary traveler, she was a seeker of beauty in a world that often felt unkind.

The next day, she made her way to the town square, where she hoped to find some information about the townspeople. She approached a group of people who were gathered around a well, gossiping and laughing.

Excuse me, she said, feeling a little nervous. I'm looking for some information about the new people who have recently moved to Lottersville. Do you know where I might find them?

The people looked at her with a mixture of curiosity and suspicion. Why do you want to know one of them asked? I..... I'm a seamstress, Seraphina said, holding up her bag. I was hoping to offer my services to the new families, and make friends as I'm also new to the town of Lottersville. I heard that there were several children in need of clothing.

The people seemed to relax a little, and one of them pointed her to the large house on the outskirts of town. That's the place, he said. The Johnson's moved in there a few days ago. They have three children, if I remember correctly.

Seraphina thanked him and set off towards the house. She couldn't wait to meet the townspeople and spread light that she had been tasked with.

When she arrived at the house, she was greeted by a kind face named Martha Johnson. She explained her mission to Martha, who was delighted to hear that Seraphina was there to help.

We've been having such a hard time finding clothes for the children, Martha said. They've grown so much since we left our old home, and we haven't had a chance to buy them new ones yet.

Seraphina spent the next few days working tirelessly, sewing clothes for the Johnson children and any other families in need. She quickly became a beloved figure in the community, and the people of Lottersville were grateful for her kindness and generosity.

But even as she worked, Seraphina couldn't shake the feeling that there was more than her just sewing clothes. She had a sense that there was something greater at stake, something she couldn't quite put her finger on. What was the light she was meant to spread and how could she do it?

She spent many nights looking up at the stars pondering these questions. She then, immediately heard a voice say if you ponder long you ponder wrong. But, she still pondered, and slowly, as the days turned into weeks, a plan began to take shape in her mind.

She would continue to help the people in Lottersville, but she would also look for ways to spread her light in other ways through out the community. She would find ways to bring hope and joy to the people who needed it most.

And so, Seraphina set out on a new journey, one that would take her to the farthest corners of the world. She knew that she would face many challenges along the way, but she was determined to fulfill her task and spread the light that had been whispered to her in the night.

# Chapter Ten

In the peaceful town of Lottersville, Seraphina who had wings as white as snow and a heart as pure as gold, was about to set off on a new angel mission. Seraphina was known far and wide for her kindness and compassion towards all living beings.

One day, as she watched over the people of Lottersville, Seraphina felt a calling deep within her soul. She knew that her purpose was to spread light and love to those in need beyond the borders of her town. With a determined heart, Seraphina bid farewell to her beloved Lottersville, and embarked on a journey to Africa.

Seraphina often spent her days watching over the people of Lottersville from her favorite perch atop a gentle hill. She would descend softly to help those in need, whether it was a child who had fallen and scraped their knee or an elderly neighbor who simply needed someone to talk to. Her laughter echoed like the sweetest melody, bringing joy to all who heard it. However, deep within her soul, she felt a calling stronger than any she had encountered before.

One evening, as the sun dipped below the horizon and painted the sky in hues of orange and purple, Seraphina sensed it an undeniable pull towards something greater. The whispers of the wind seemed to carry the voices of those in distant lands, pleading for help. It was then she knew her purpose extended beyond the borders of Lottersville. There were others out there who needed her light, her love, and her caring touch.

With a determined heart, she bid farewell to her beloved town. The townsfolk gathered to send her off, their faces a mixture of pride and sorrow. Children waved tiny flags, and adults embraced her one last time, tears glistening in their eyes. Come back to us, they whispered, but Seraphina knew this was a journey she must take.

As she soared through the sky, the world beneath her transformed from the familiar landscapes of Lottersville into vast stretches of golden savannah and dense jungles. Her heart raced with anticipation and excitement. She had heard of the beauty and struggles of Africa, and she was eager to lend her wings to those who needed them most.

Upon her arrival, she found herself in a small village surrounded by lush greenery but marred by the scars of hardship. The villagers greeted her with a mixture of awe and fear, for they had never seen a creature so ethereal. Seraphina introduced herself, her voice gentle and soothing. She explained her mission, to bring hope, healing, and compassion to those in need.

In Africa, Seraphina found herself in a bustling village where people were in need of hope and help. Guided by her instincts, she began to use her talents as a seamstress to create beautiful garments for the villagers. Her hands worked tirelessly, weaving threads of love and compassion into every stitch.

Not only did Seraphina excel in her seamstress work, but she also dedicated herself to charitable deeds. She helped the villagers build homes, provided food for the hungry, and tended to the sick and needy. Her presence brought a sense of peace and joy to the community, and her light shone brightly in the darkest of times.

Days turned into weeks, weeks into months, and Seraphina's presence in Africa became a beacon of hope for all who crossed her path. Through her selfless acts of kindness and unwavering dedication, she touched the lives of countless people and inspired them to keep faith in brighter tomorrows.

And so, the story of Seraphina, the angel who left Lottersville to spread light in Africa through her seamstress work and charity, became a legend told by generations to come, reminding everyone of the power of love and compassion in changing the world for the better.

Days turned into weeks as Seraphina immersed herself in the lives of the villagers. She helped tend to the sick, gather food, and teach children who had never set foot in a classroom. Her laughter blended with the sounds of the village, and slowly, the fear in their eyes was replaced with warmth and trust. She felt fulfilled, believing she was truly making a difference.

However, amidst the joy and laughter, there were shadows. One day, she met a little girl named Amelia, who had lost her parents to a tragic illness. Amelia's eyes were filled with sorrow, her spirit dimmed by loss. Seraphina instantly felt a connection to the child, understanding her pain in a way that words could not express. She spent hours with Amelia sharing stories and dreams, trying to bring light back into her life.

Yet, for Seraphina, the weight of the world began to press down on her heart. Each night, she would gaze at the stars, wishing she could do more. She often thought of Lottersville and the people she had left behind. The laughter of children there felt like a distant memory, replaced by the haunting silence of Amelia's tears.

One fateful day, tragedy struck the town. A sudden illness swept through, claiming lives and leaving many in despair. Seraphina worked tirelessly, using all her strength to heal the sick and comfort the grieving. But despite her efforts, she watched helplessly as Amelia succumbed to the very illness that had taken her parents. The little girl's fragile body lay still, her spirit finally at peace, leaving a void that could not be filled.

The loss shattered Seraphina's heart. She had come to bring light and joy, but instead, she had witnessed the darkest corners of humanity's suffering. The town, once filled with hope, fell into mourning, and Seraphina felt the weight of her mission crushing her. She had failed to save Amelia, and with her, the light that had flickered in the village dimmed.

In the solitude of her sorrow, Seraphina took flight and soared high above the clouds, seeking solace among the stars. She cried out to the heavens, asking why she had been sent on this mission only to witness such pain. As her tears fell like raindrops, she felt a gentle warmth envelop her a comforting embrace from the universe reminding her that even in the depths of despair, hope could still blossom.

Returning to the town, Seraphina resolved to honor Amelia's memory. She gathered the townspeople, sharing stories of the little girl's laughter, dreams, and the love she had for her community. They created a memorial, a beautiful garden filled with flowers that symbolized Amelia's spirit vibrant, resilient, and full of life. Seraphina encouraged them to continue nurturing that spirit, to keep the light alive in their hearts.

Over time, the town began to heal. They learned to lean on one another in their grief, finding strength in community. Seraphina, too, found healing in their resilience. She realized that while she could not prevent all suffering, she could offer companionship in pain and joy in remembrance.

Though she would always carry Amelia's memory in her heart, she vowed to keep spreading love and light. As she prepared to return to Lottersville, the townspeople gathered to bid her farewell, their hearts now filled with gratitude instead of sorrow. They had learned that even amidst loss, hope could flourish, and love had the power to transcend boundaries.

With a final glance back at the town, Seraphina took to the skies, her wings shining brighter than ever, carrying with her the stories of those she had touched and the lessons of love and resilience. She flew home, knowing that her mission was far from over. There would always be another soul in need, another heart to heal, and she would always answer the call.

# Chapter Eleven

Seraphina had always been a spirited young woman, eager to explore the world and make a difference. So, when she embarked on a journey to Africa to volunteer and do charity work, she was filled with enthusiasm and optimism.

For the first few weeks, Seraphina threw herself into her work, helping the local community, building schools, and providing much needed aid. The people she met touched her heart, and their resilience inspired her to do more. However, as the weeks turned into months, Seraphina began to feel a growing sense of weariness creeping into her bones.

Each passing day, she found herself thinking more and more about her hometown of Lottersville. Memories of lazy afternoons by the river, the familiar faces of her neighbors, and the comforting embrace of her family called out to her. The bustling streets of Africa, while vibrant and alive, seemed to grow lonelier with each passing day.

Seraphina missed the simple joys of home the smell of her home town cooking, the sound of children playing in the streets, and the warmth of her own bed. As she sat under the African sky, surrounded by strangers who had become friends, she realized that what she truly longed for was the familiarity and comfort of home.

And so, with a heavy heart but a deep sense of gratitude for her time in Africa, Seraphina made the decision to return to Lottersville. She knew that she had made a difference in the lives of many people during her time abroad, but now it was time to recharge, to rest, and to find solace in the arms of her loved ones once again.

As she boarded the plane back to her hometown, Seraphina felt a mix of emotions, excitement to see her family and friends again, sadness to leave behind the new life she had built in Africa, and a sense of relief to be returning to familiar surroundings. The memories of her time abroad would always hold a special place in her heart, but she knew that home was where she truly belonged.

Upon arriving in Lottersville, Seraphina was greeted with open arms by her family and friends. The familiar sights and sounds of her hometown enveloped her, bringing a sense of peace and contentment that she had been longing for. As she walked through the streets, she felt a deep sense of belonging and connection that she had missed during her time away.

Reconnecting with her neighbors and loved ones, Seraphina found herself falling back into the rhythms of daily life in Lottersville. The simple pleasures of home, sharing meals with her family, chatting with old friends at the local market, and taking leisurely strolls along the river brought her a sense of joy and fulfillment that she had been missing in Africa.

As she settled back into her old routines, Seraphina reflected on her time abroad and the impact she had made on the lives of those she had met in Africa. While she had experienced personal growth and had made a difference in the lives of others, she realized that her true happiness lay in the familiar comforts and connections of home. Each passing day, she found herself feeling more grateful for the experiences she had had, but also more certain that Lottersville was where she belonged.

# Chapter Twelve

As she walked through the familiar streets, she couldn't contain her excitement to reunite with her dear friend Martha Johnson and her three children.

When Seraphina finally reached Martha's cozy home, she was warmly welcomed with open arms. The sweet smiles of Martha's children filled her heart with joy, and she was taken aback by the mouth watering aroma wafting from the kitchen.

As they sat down to eat, Seraphina was pleasantly surprised by the delicious feast that Martha and her children had prepared for her. The table was filled with an array of tempting dishes, lovingly crafted with care and consideration. Seraphina couldn't help but feel overwhelmed with gratitude for such a thoughtful gesture.

As they sat around the table, Seraphina couldn't help but admire the effort and love that Martha and her children had put into preparing the meal. The aroma of spices and herbs filled the air, enticing her taste buds and stirring memories of home cooked meals from her childhood. Each dish was a masterpiece in its own right, showcasing the culinary skills and creativity of her dear friends.

As the evening progressed, Seraphina found herself opening up to Martha and her children in a way she hadn't expected. The shared meal became a symbol of the bond they shared, a connection that transcended distance and time apart. The laughter and chatter that filled the room were like music to Seraphina's ears, soothing her soul and filling her heart with joy.

Through the stories and anecdotes shared around the table, Seraphina felt a sense of belonging that she had missed during her time away. The warmth and comfort of friendship surrounded her, reminding her of the importance of human connection and the value of shared experiences. In that moment, she realized just how much she had missed the simple pleasures of companionship and camaraderie.

As the night wore on, Seraphina found herself feeling grateful for the kindness and generosity shown to her by Martha and her children. The feast they had prepared was not just a meal, but a gesture of love and care that touched her deeply. It was a reminder of the power of food to bring people together, to nourish not just the body but also the soul.

As they finished their meal, Seraphina knew that she would always treasure the memories of that evening spent with her friends. The laughter, the stories, the delicious food all of it had rekindled a spark within her, reminding her of the importance of cherishing the moments of connection and joy in life. With a heart full of gratitude, she thanked Martha and her children for a truly unforgettable evening.

Throughout the evening, laughter filled the air as Seraphina and her friends shared stories and caught up on lost time. The warmth of friendship and love enveloped them, creating a sense of belonging and happiness that Seraphina had missed dearly during her time away.

As the night grew darker and the stars twinkled in the sky, Seraphina realized that true happiness lies in the simple moments shared with loved ones. With a heart full of gratitude and a soul nourished by friendship, Seraphina knew that she was truly home in Lottersville, surrounded by the people who cared for her the most.

# Chapter Thirteen

Seraphina had just bid farewell to Martha and her children after a wonderful visit in the neighboring town. As she made her way back to Lottersville, the familiarity of the winding roads and quaint countryside sights filled her with a sense of comfort and joy. Thoughts of her cozy home awaited her, where her bed felt like a sanctuary after being away for months.

Upon reaching Lottersville, the sun was beginning to set, casting a warm orange hue over the town. Seraphina could already picture the inviting glow emanating from her cottage windows. She hastened her steps, feeling eager at the thought of sinking into her soft, familiar bed.

Finally reaching her home, Seraphina pushed open the creaky wooden door and stepped inside. The quiet of her cottage welcomed her like an old friend. The scent of wildflowers from her garden wafted through the open window, mingling with the gentle evening breeze.

Seraphina made her way to her bedroom, her steps light with anticipation. As she entered the room, she couldn't help but smile at the sight of her cozy bed, adorned with soft pillows and a thick, warm quilt. The fatigue from her journey seemed to melt away at the mere sight of it.

With a contented sigh, Seraphina lowered herself onto the bed, feeling the softness envelop her tired body. The familiar comfort of her own bed was like a hug from home itself. Nestling into the familiar sheets, she closed her eyes, feeling grateful for her safe return and the simple joy of being back in her own haven.

As Seraphina drifted off to sleep, surrounded by the comfort of her home, she knew that no matter how far she traveled, her bed in Lottersville would always be the sweetest place to rest her head.

Seraphina had made a heartfelt promise to visit Martha's home the following day, eager to help her friend with a pressing need. With Martha's children growing at an astonishing rate, their wardrobes had become a patchwork of ill fitting garments, and Seraphina was determined to create new clothes that would not only fit them perfectly but also reflect their vibrant personalities.

The following day, Seraphina arrived at Martha's home with a bag filled with fabrics, threads, and patterns, ready to embark on her mission to create new clothes for her friend's children. The excitement in Martha's eyes mirrored Seraphina's own enthusiasm, as they set to work transforming the mismatched garments into stylish and well fitting outfits that would bring a smile to the children's faces.

As the sound of the sewing machine hummed in the background, Seraphina and Martha measured, cut, and stitched with precision and care, each garment taking shape under their skilled hands. The collaborative effort and shared passion for creating something beautiful filled the room with a sense of joy and purpose, strengthening the bond between the two friends.

With each stitch, Seraphina poured her heart and soul into the project, infusing the clothes with love, creativity, and attention to detail. The vibrant fabrics and playful designs reflected the personalities of Martha's children, capturing their spirit and individuality in every seam and hem. Seraphina's dedication to making sure the clothes fit perfectly was a testament to her commitment to bringing joy and comfort to those she cared about.

As the day wore on, the living room was transformed into a makeshift workshop, with patterns and fabrics strewn about and the air filled with the scent of freshly ironed cloth. Despite the hard work and concentration required, laughter and shared stories flowed freely between Seraphina and Martha, creating a sense of joy and excitement that made the task feel more like a joyous celebration of friendship than a chore.

By the end of the day, as the last button was sewn and the final hem was pressed, Seraphina and Martha looked upon the finished garments with pride and satisfaction. The clothes not only fit perfectly but also radiated a sense of love and care that could be felt in every stitch. As they admired their handiwork, Seraphina knew that she had fulfilled her promise to her friend and had created something truly special that would be cherished by Martha's children for years to come.

# Chapter Fourteen

The next morning, with the sun casting a golden hue over the landscape, Seraphina stepped out of her cozy cottage, ready to embark on her short journey to Martha's home. Dressed in a flowing sundress adorned with colorful patterns reminiscent of the vibrant markets she had visited in Africa, she took a moment to breathe in the fresh, fragrant air. The wildflower field beside her was a riot of colors, and she couldn't resist pausing to admire the delicate petals dancing in the gentle breeze.

With a smile on her face, Seraphina continued her walk, her heart light with anticipation. The thought of sharing more adventures with Martha excited her. However, as she crossed the road, her gaze still lingering on the wildflowers, tragedy struck. A car, speeding down the road, came around the bend too quickly for the driver to notice her presence.

In an instant, the world around her turned chaotic. The screech of tires and the blaring horn filled the air as Seraphina was knocked off her feet. Time seemed to slow as she felt the impact, and then everything went dark.

As Seraphina tried to piece together what had happened, a wave of fear and uncertainty washed over her. The realization of the accident and the gravity of her injuries hit her like a ton of bricks. Despite the pain and confusion, her thoughts immediately turned to her loved ones, especially Martha and the children. She longed to see their faces, to reassure them that she was okay and to continue the adventures they had planned.

As the hours passed, Seraphina was visited by doctors and nurses who explained the extent of her injuries and the road to recovery that lay ahead. The news was sobering, but Seraphina's determination and resilience shone through. She knew that the road to recovery would be long and arduous, but she was determined to overcome the challenges and emerge stronger on the other side.

In the quiet moments of the hospital room, Seraphina found solace in memories of her time spent with Martha and the children. The thought of their laughter, their shared adventures, and the bond of friendship they had formed gave her strength and hope. Despite the pain and uncertainty of her current situation, she held onto the promise of brighter days ahead, filled with new adventures and cherished moments with her dear friends.

As Seraphina lay in her hospital bed, surrounded by the beeping machines and sterile walls, she felt a deep sense of gratitude for the love and support of those who cared for her. The thought of Martha and the children waiting for her on the other side of recovery motivated her to push through the pain and to focus on healing. She knew that the road ahead would be tough, but with the love and friendship that surrounded her, she felt confident that she would emerge stronger and ready to continue.

As days passed, and the news of Seraphina's accident spread through Lottersville like wildfire. Martha, devastated by the news, rushed to the hospital, her heart heavy with worry. When she arrived, she found Seraphina awake, albeit weak and bandaged.

Oh, Seraphina! Martha exclaimed, tears streaming down her face as she rushed to her friend's side. I was so worried! I thought I'd lost you!

Seraphina managed a weak smile, her eyes sparkling with resilience. I'm here, Martha. I'm still here. Just a little banged up, that's all.

As the two friends sat together, sharing stories of courage and hope, a nurse entered the room. She brought with her a bouquet of wildflowers, vibrant and cheerful, brightening the sterile surroundings. These were delivered for you, Seraphina. They're from the townspeople of Lottersville, the nurse said, placing the flowers on the bedside table.

Tears welled up in Seraphina's eyes as she inhaled the sweet fragrance of the wildflowers. They reminded her of the beauty of life, of the friendships that mattered most, and the adventures that still awaited her. Thank you, she whispered, her heart swelling with gratitude.

With Martha by her side, Seraphina began to heal, both physically and emotionally. The accident had been a tragedy, but it also revealed the strength of their friendship and the love of their community. As she recovered, she found solace in the stories she had collected during her travels, weaving them into the fabric of her life.

Eventually, Seraphina returned home, stronger than ever, and with a newfound appreciation for each moment. She and Martha worked together, creating beautiful garments for the children, each stitch infused with love and resilience. The wildflower field became a symbol of hope, reminding them both that even after tragedy, beauty could still bloom.

# Chapter Fifteen

In the quaint little town of Lottersville nestled between rolling hills and shimmering streams, there lived two extraordinary friends, Seraphina and Martha. Seraphina was known for her ethereal beauty and gentle spirit, often likened to a celestial being. Martha, on the other hand, was a warm hearted mother of three rapidly growing children whose laughter could light up even the gloomiest of days.

For years, the two friends spent countless hours together, sewing clothes for Martha's children. As they stitched and chatted, they shared their hopes, dreams, and fears. It was during these moments that Seraphina discovered the true essence of friendship. She realized that even angels, like herself, need the support of others to soar.

One fateful day, as Seraphina was out gathering flowers for a special bouquet, she met with an unfortunate accident. A sudden storm swept through the town, another accident she heard a faint whisper say as she tried to find shelter, she slipped and fell, injuring her ankle. The pain was sharp and immediate, and for the first time, Seraphina felt the weight of vulnerability.

In the aftermath of the accident, Martha was by Seraphina's side in an instant, her warm presence and caring touch a comforting balm to Seraphina's pain. Martha's children, too, rallied around their beloved friend, offering words of encouragement and small gestures of kindness that lifted Seraphina's spirits. In that moment of vulnerability, Seraphina found strength in the unwavering support and love of her friends.

As Seraphina recovered from her injury, she found herself reflecting on the fragility of life and the importance of cherishing the moments spent with loved ones. The accident had been a stark reminder of how quickly circumstances can change, but it had also reaffirmed the bond of friendship that she shared with

Martha and her children. Seraphina felt a deep sense of gratitude for the love and care that had surrounded her in her time of need.

Together, Seraphina and Martha navigated the challenges of recovery, drawing strength from each other's presence and the shared memories of their friendship. As they sat together, stitching clothes and sharing stories, Seraphina realized that true friendship was not just about the good times but also about being there for each other during the difficult moments. The accident had brought them closer, deepening their bond and reinforcing the importance of being there for one another through thick and thin.

In the days that followed, Seraphina's ankle healed, and she was able to walk again, albeit with a slight limp. The experience had left a mark on her, a reminder of her own vulnerability and the fragility of life. But it had also strengthened her resolve to cherish the moments spent with Martha and the children, to continue sewing clothes and sharing stories, and to nurture the extraordinary friendship that had blossomed between them in the quaint little town of Lottersville.

As Seraphina looked out over the rolling hills and shimmering streams of Lottersville, she felt a profound sense of gratitude for the friendship she shared with Martha and her children. In their laughter, their shared moments of joy and sorrow, and their unwavering support, Seraphina had found a kind of beauty and strength that transcended earthly bounds. Together, they would continue to sew the fabric of their friendship, stitching together moments of love, laughter, and companionship that would endure for years to come.

One evening, as they sat by the fire, Seraphina turned to Martha, her eyes sparkling with gratitude. You are my angel, Martha. I don't think I would have healed so quickly if it weren't for you. Even angels need other angels.

Martha smiled, her cheeks flushed with warmth. "And you are mine, Seraphina. You remind me that I, too, need help sometimes. We all do. It's okay not to be perfect, and it's okay to lean on each other.

From that day forward, the bond between the two friends deepened. They became each other's wings, lifting one another up in times of need. Seraphina learned that vulnerability was not a weakness but a path to greater strength, especially when shared with someone who truly cared. Martha discovered that her kindness could create ripples of healing, not just in her own heart but in the hearts of those around her.

As the seasons changed, so did their lives. They continued to sew beautiful clothes, but now they also stitched together moments of joy, laughter, and love. The town of Lottersville, soon recognized the magic of their friendship, and it inspired others to reach out and support one another in their own struggles.

In the end, Seraphina and Martha understood that while they were both angels in their own right, it was their connection that truly made them shine. They became a testament to the power of friendship a reminder that even the most celestial beings need a helping hand, and that together, they could weather any storm.

# Chapter 16

In the town of Lottersville, where the sun painted the skies with hues of orange and pink at dusk, lived two inseparable friends: Seraphina and Martha. They had grown through many trials and obstacles together, sharing laughter, dreams, and secrets beneath the sprawling branches of the ancient oak tree that stood at the heart of their town.

Seraphina was known for her radiant spirit. Her laughter was like a melody that could brighten the gloomiest of days, and her kindness knew no bounds. Martha, on the other hand, was the thinker of the duo. She had a curious mind, always seeking knowledge and understanding the world around her. Together, they balanced each other perfectly, like the sun and the moon.

One day, while sitting under their beloved oak, in the field of wildflowers, Seraphina turned to Martha with a sparkle in her eyes. What if we could spread our light beyond Lottersville together? She proposed, her voice bubbling with excitement. What if we could share our joy and kindness with the world?

Martha pondered for a moment, her brow furrowing in thought. It sounds wonderful, but how do we start?

With a determined smile, Seraphina jumped to her feet. We'll embark on a journey! We can create a series of small acts of kindness and share them with everyone we meet. We'll inspire others to do the same!

And so, the two friends set off on their adventure, armed with nothing but their hearts full of hope and a small satchel filled with supplies. Their first stop was the town square in Lottersville, where they noticed a group of children playing in a dusty square.

Let's bring them some joy Seraphina exclaimed. They gathered the children and organized a makeshift game, teaching them how to play tag and sharing stories of their own childhood escapades. Laughter echoed through the square, and for a moment, the worries of the world faded away.

As the sun began to set over the field of wildflowers, Seraphina and Martha sat side by side, their hearts full of excitement and determination. The idea of spreading their light and kindness beyond the borders of Lottersville filled them with a sense of purpose and joy. Together, they envisioned a world filled with love, compassion, and goodwill, and they were eager to take the first step on their journey.

With a newfound sense of purpose, Seraphina and Martha began brainstorming ideas for their series of small acts of kindness. They talked about ways to brighten someone's day, spread positivity, and make a difference in the lives of others. Each idea sparked a new wave of enthusiasm and creativity, as they envisioned the ripple effect of their actions reaching far and wide, touching hearts and inspiring others to join in their mission.

As they crafted their plan, Seraphina and Martha felt a deep sense of connection and unity. Their shared vision of spreading joy and kindness became a beacon of light that guided them forward, fueling their determination to make a positive impact on the world. With each idea they shared and each detail they worked out, their friendship grew stronger, bound by a shared passion for making the world a better place.

As the days turned into weeks, Seraphina and Martha set out on their journey, armed with kindness, love, and a desire to make a difference. They started small, performing random acts of kindness in their own community, from helping a neighbor with groceries to planting flowers in the town square. With each act, they saw the smiles on people's faces, felt the warmth in their hearts, and knew that they were spreading light in a world that often felt dark.

As they continued on their path, Seraphina and Martha encountered challenges and obstacles, but their bond and determination never wavered. They found strength in each other, in the shared moments of triumph and resilience, and in the belief that together, they could truly make a difference. With every act of kindness, every smile shared, and every hand extended in friendship, Seraphina and Martha were spreading their light beyond Lottersville, touching hearts and inspiring others to join them on their journey of love and compassion.

As they continued their journey, Seraphina and Martha encountered many people in need. They visited the elderly at a nearby nursing home, bringing flowers and singing cheerful songs. They helped farmers in the fields, lending a hand and sharing smiles as they worked side by side. Each act of kindness sparked joy not only in those they helped but also within themselves.

One evening, as the sun dipped below the horizon, painting the sky with stars, the friends found themselves camping under a vast canopy of twinkling lights. Martha gazed up at the stars, her heart swelling with happiness. "I never knew spreading light could feel this good," she whispered.

Seraphina nodded, her eyes shining. "We're not just spreading light, Martha. We're creating ripples of kindness that will inspire others to shine too."

Their journey took them to distant towns and bustling cities, where they met people from all walks of life. They listened to their stories and shared their own, weaving a tapestry of connection that transcended boundaries. With each act of kindness, they inspired others to join their cause, and soon, their movement began to grow.

Days passed, and the duo returned to Lottersville, transformed by their experiences. They had spread their light far and wide, but they realized that their journey was far from over. They decided to host a festival in their town, inviting everyone they had met along the way.

On the day of the festival, the town square was filled with laughter, music, and the aroma of delicious food. People from different towns came together, sharing stories of kindness they had experienced and how they had continued the chain of goodwill.

As the sun set, Seraphina and Martha stood hand in hand, watching the vibrant celebration unfold. "Look at all the light we've created," Martha said, her voice filled with awe.

Seraphina smiled, her heart swelling with pride. And it all started with a simple idea two friends wanting to make the world a better place for all.

# Chapter Seventeen

As the sun began to dip below the horizon, casting a warm glow over the quaint town , Seraphina and Martha exchanged lingering glances filled with shared excitement and contentment. The festival had been a whirlwind of laughter, music, and vibrant colors, enveloping them in a magical atmosphere that seemed to transport them far from their everyday lives. Yet, as the joyous sounds of the celebration faded into the distance, a wave of calm washed over them, beckoning them back to the familiar solace of their homes. Each step toward their front doors was a reminder of the cherished moments they had just experienced, and they knew these memories would be a source of joy for many days to come.

For Seraphina, her home was a sanctuary filled with the loving echoes of family and the comforting scent of her grandmother's baked goods that lingered in the air. As she entered, the warmth embraced her like a gentle hug, and the soft glow of the evening lights welcomed her back to the world of familiarity. The gentle hum of her family's voices drifted from the kitchen, where discussions about the festival blended seamlessly with the clattering of pots and pans. She felt a delightful anticipation swell in her heart, knowing that soon she would be sharing the day's adventures over dinner, with laughter weaving through the stories told.

Meanwhile, Martha stepped into her cozy abode, where the soothing rustle of some well-loved books awaited her. She took a moment to soak in the tranquility that surrounded her, appreciating the way her home was adorned with memories of past celebrations. The walls were lined with photographs of family gatherings, and colorful handmade decorations from festivals gone by. As she settled into her favorite armchair by the window, the gentle flicker of candlelight illuminated her serene space, creating a cocoon of warmth where she could reflect on the day. The festival had been exhilarating, yet here was a different kind of joy one rooted in stillness and the comfort of her cherished belongings.

Both women found themselves savoring the newfound stillness after the whirlwind of the festival. In the quiet of their homes, they began to sift through the colorful fabric of their memories, recounting the exhilarating moments the spectacular fireworks display, the laughter shared with friends, and the delight of tasting treats crafted by local artisans. With each fond remembrance, their hearts swelled with gratitude for the connections and experiences that had enriched their lives. It was in these simple recollections that they found growth and warmth, bridging the gaps between moments of celebration and the mundanity that often followed.

As night descended, the stars twinkled brightly overhead, and while Seraphina and Martha might have been separated by a few streets, they shared an unspoken bond fortified by the festival's joy. Each in their own home, they settled into a sense of peace, grateful for the life they were building in their beloved town. Together, they created a tapestry stitched with threads of love, laughter, and memories, a reminder that although festivals come to an end, the spirit of celebration and unity continues to dwell in their hearts, weaving together the fabric of their lives as they moved into a new day.

As Seraphina and Martha hurried back home from the festival, their hearts were heavy with the weight of the joy they had shared with so many. The light they had spread far and wide now seemed to dim as they longed for the comfort of their own beds and the familiarity of their homes.

For days, they had been the bearers of happiness, their smiles brightening the faces of everyone they met in Lottersville and beyond. But as the festival came to an end, the exhaustion of constant cheerfulness began to take its toll.

Martha, especially, felt the pull of home growing stronger with each passing moment. Her three children awaited her return eagerly, their little faces etched in her mind as she quickened her pace, eager to hold them close once more.

The journey back seemed longer than the one they had made to the festival grounds. The road stretched out endlessly before them, the setting sun casting long shadows across their path. Seraphina and Martha walked in silence, their steps heavy with fatigue and the weight of all they had experienced.

As they finally reached the outskirts of Lottersville, the familiar sights and sounds of home greeted them like old friends. The laughter of children playing in the streets, the smell of home-cooked meals wafting through the air – it was a bittersweet reminder of the life they had temporarily left behind.

And as they entered their respective homes, Seraphina and Martha knew that the memories of the festival would linger in their hearts for a long time to come. But for now, all they craved was the simple comfort of being home, surrounded by the ones they loved.

# Chapter Eighteen

Seraphina stood in her dimly lit living room, the words hanging heavy in the air like a thick fog. The faint whisper lingered in her ears, whispering with a haunting tone that seemed to seep into her very soul. When are you going to start a family? The question reverberated in her mind, stirring up a storm of emotions that she had long kept buried.

As she gazed at the flickering candle flames, the words that had been spoken earlier continued to echo in her mind, wrapping around her thoughts like a heavy shroud. When are you going to start a family? The voice that had posed the question was soft but penetrating, igniting a flicker of anger and sadness within her. This probing inquiry triggered a flood of memories, swirling like autumn leaves caught in a windstorm, and she couldn't shake the haunting feeling that it was a question loaded with expectations and societal norms she wasn't sure she could fulfill.

At thirty three years old, Seraphina felt the weight of the world resting squarely on her shoulders. The invisible clock of her life ticked loudly in her ears, reminding her of all the milestones that expected to have arrived at by now. The idea of family had always seemed like a blissful dream, a horizon she could always see but never quite reach. As she reflected on her journey thus far, she identified the countless moments she had prioritized the needs of others over her own, dutifully stepping into the role of caretaker for friends and family. Her heart ached as she confronted the reality that those selfless choices had come at the cost of her own desires and aspirations she had unknowingly become a guardian of others' happiness while neglecting her own.

As the storm of emotions swirled within her, Seraphina felt a sharp pang of regret cut through the haze. She had often derided her own ambitions, perpetually placing her dreams on a shelf marked later. The vibrant visions she had for her future rising in her career, traveling to far-off lands, or even cultivating a loving relationship had been dulled by the incessant duties she had shouldered. She realized now that in prioritizing everyone else's well-being, she had lost sight of who she was and what she truly wanted. The questions of motherhood and family felt both tantalizing and terrifying, a reflection of the life she had long envisioned for herself but had never actively pursued.

In that moment, Seraphina gained clarity. It wasn't too late to change the narrative of her life. The candlelight illuminated her reflection in the window, and she recognized a fierce determination brewing within her. It was time to rewrite her story, to step into the forefront of her own life rather than perpetually standing in the background. No longer would she allow herself to be defined by the expectations of others or bound by the insecurities that had held her captive for so long. She was ready to embrace the possibility of motherhood not as an obligation but as a choice a chapter she could write when she felt ready and worthy of such fulfillment.

As the night deepened and the comforting stillness engulfed her home, Seraphina made a silent promise to herself. She would embark on a journey of self discovery, uncovering her true passions and desires. The question that had haunted her earlier now served as a catalyst for introspection and empowerment. The future remained unwritten, and she would navigate it on her own terms selecting which paths to pursue and when to take the leap into the unknown. For the first time in a long while, she felt a flicker of hope igniting within her a reminder that while the choices she had made shaped her past, her future was still a canvass waiting for her to paint it vibrant with the colors.

Seraphina had spent so much of her life tending to the needs of others, sacrificing her own desires and dreams in the process. The realization hit her like a bolt of lightning she had neglected herself for far too long, always putting everyone else first.

The memory of her dear friend Lysander, now gone from this world, added a new layer of sorrow to her already heavy heart. He had been her confidant, her rock, her guiding light in times of darkness. The thought of never finding someone like him again left a gaping hole in her chest, a void that seemed impossible to fill.

As Seraphina grappled with these conflicting emotions, she questioned whether she was truly ready to open her heart to another. The fear of facing loss once more, the uncertainty of starting anew, it all seemed too overwhelming. But deep down, a flicker of hope remained - a glimmer of possibility that whispered, The only way to know is to try.

And so, with a heavy heart and a hesitant spirit, Seraphina took a tentative step forward into the unknown. The path ahead was shrouded in shadows, but somewhere in the darkness, a sliver of light beckoned her to keep moving, to keep searching for the answers she sought.

The journey towards self discovery and healing had only just begun for Seraphina, but with each step she took, she found a strength she never knew she possessed. And as she navigated the twists and turns of her own heart, she knew that whatever lay ahead, she would face it with courage and resilience, knowing that the only way to find true happiness was to first learn to love herself.

# Chapter Nineteen

Seraphina's heart ached with a longing she had kept buried deep within her for years. The desire to find someone to share her life with, to start a family, to feel that deep connection with another soul. She confided in her dear friend Martha, sharing her hopes and fears. And when Martha mentioned the young doctor, a friend of her husband's, Seraphina felt a glimmer of hope flicker within her.

But Martha's words stung as she mentioned Lysander's tragedy, a painful memory that Seraphina had kept locked away. The wounds of the past still raw, the loss of Lysander haunting her every step. Yet, Martha's happiness and encouragement sparked a light of possibility in Seraphina's heart.

Could she dare to hope again? To let someone new into her life, to open her heart to the possibility of love and happiness once more? Despite the lingering shadows of the past, Seraphina found herself nodding, a tentative smile playing on her lips.

Martha's offer to set her up on a date with the young doctor filled Seraphina with a mix of excitement and trepidation. Could this be the start of something new, something beautiful? Or would it only lead to more heartache and pain?

As Seraphina contemplated Martha's offer, a swirl of emotions and memories flooded her mind. The journey ahead was uncertain, the path unknown. But deep within her, a glimmer of hope blossomed, a tiny seed of possibility taking root.

Martha's enthusiastic suggestion to set Seraphina up with the young doctor sent a jolt of mixed emotions through her. Excitement coursed through her veins, igniting a spark she hadn't felt in what seemed like an eternity. The prospect of meeting someone new, of potentially finding a connection that could blossom into something meaningful, made her heart race with anticipation. Yet, interwoven with that excitement was a thread of trepidation. Seraphina couldn't help but question whether this new venture was a courageous leap into the unknown or just a gateway to further heartache and disappointment, a reminder of the love she once craved but had long stopped believing in.

As Seraphina sat in her dimly lit living room, she found herself lost in contemplation, a swirl of emotions and memories enveloping her like a soft, familiar blanket. She recalled past relationships that had burned brightly only to fizzle out, leaving behind aching voids and lingering what ifs. Each experience brought a lesson, often engraved with the pain of unfulfilled dreams or unmet expectations. With those memories whispering in the corners of her mind, she grappled with the uncertainty of opening her heart once again. Could she allow herself to hope for something beautiful, or was the specter of past disappointments too great to overcome?

Yet, amid the uncertainty, a glimmer of hope began to unfurl within her. It was faint at first, as if a tiny seed was taking root a beautiful possibility nestled deep in her heart. The idea of stepping outside her comfort zone and embracing a new chapter was both terrifying and exhilarating. Seraphina recognized that she could no longer wait for the perfect moment; perhaps this could be her moment for growth and joy. Quietly, she resolved to embrace the journey ahead, knowing it might be filled with ups and downs. What mattered most was that she was ready to take a chance, to allow herself the chance to love and be loved in return, even if it meant facing the uncertainties that came with it.

Seraphina took a deep breath, her heart heavy with the weight of the past, yet light with the possibility of the future. With Martha's words echoing in her ears, she made a decision to take a chance, to embark on this new journey of love and hope.

And so, with a mix of fear and anticipation, Seraphina stepped forward into the unknown, ready to embrace whatever fate had in store for her. The journey of finding someone to share her life with had begun, and Seraphina was determined to see where it would lead.

# Chapter Twenty

Seraphina felt a nervous excitement as she prepared for her first date with Dr. Richard. Their evening was planned to start with a cozy dinner at a trendy restaurant, followed by a visit to a comedy show in the heart of the city. As she stepped out of her home, she couldn't help but feel a sense of anticipation for what the night held in store.

Dr. Richard greeted her with a warm smile, and Seraphina found herself immediately at ease in his presence. Their conversation flowed effortlessly as they savored their meal, sharing stories and laughter over candlelight. Seraphina was struck by Dr. Richard's intelligence and wit, finding herself drawn to his charm and charisma.

The comedy show proved to be the perfect follow up to their dinner, with both Seraphina and Dr. Richard enjoying the humor and levity of the performances. As they walked out of the theater, Seraphina realized that she felt a deep connection with Dr. Richard, a sense of understanding and companionship that she had never experienced before.

The night continued with spontaneous detours and unexpected discoveries, from late night strolls in the city to sharing childhood memories over cups of hot chocolate. Seraphina found herself opening up to Dr. Richard in a way she had never done with anyone else, feeling a sense of trust and comfort that was both exhilarating and comforting.

The night unfolded with a sense of adventure as Seraphina and Dr. Richard embarked on spontaneous detours through the city. Their late night strolls led them to hidden corners and vibrant streets, where the ambient sounds of the nightlife created a backdrop for their exploration. Each unexpected discovery, from quaint cafes to lively street performances, added a layer of excitement to their evening, transforming the mundane into memorable experiences. The city, alive with energy, mirrored the growing connection between them, as they shared laughter and stories under the stars.

As they settled into a cozy cafe, cups of hot chocolate in hand, the atmosphere shifted from playful exploration to heartfelt conversation. Seraphina found herself reminiscing about childhood memories, sharing tales that had long been tucked away. This openness surprised her, she had never felt such a level of trust with anyone before. Dr. Richard listened intently, his warm demeanor encouraging her to delve deeper into her past, revealing vulnerabilities she had kept hidden. The comfort of their shared moments allowed her to explore feelings of exhilaration and safety, creating a unique bond between them.

In this intimate setting, Seraphina realized that her connection with Dr. Richard was unlike any other. The combination of late night adventures and heartfelt exchanges fostered a sense of belonging and understanding that she had yearned for. Each shared memory and spontaneous detour solidified their growing friendship, leaving Seraphina both exhilarated and comforted by the connection they were forging. The night became a tapestry of experiences, weaving together trust, laughter, and the promise of deeper exploration in the days to come.

By the end of the night, as they said their goodbyes outside Seraphina's home, she knew that this was just the beginning of something special. As she watched Dr. Richard walk away, a smile played on her lips, knowing that she had found not just a date, but a kindred spirit and a true connection that promised a future filled with love and laughter.

# Chapter Twenty One

Seraphina couldn't stop smiling as she recounted her first meeting with Dr. Richard's to her dear friend Martha. I can't believe you set me up on this first date, Martha! I can't thank you enough, Seraphina gushed with excitement.

Martha smiled back at her, her eyes gleaming with excitement and happiness. I knew you two would hit it off, Seraphina. I could just feel it.

Seraphina nodded, her mind still reeling from the instant connection she had felt with Dr. Richards's. It was like we were old friends, Martha. We talked for hours about everything our hopes, our dreams, our fears. It was like he truly saw me, you know?

Martha reached out and squeezed Seraphina's hand. I'm so glad, Seraphina. You deserve to be seen and loved for who you truly are. Seraphina felt a lump form in her throat. Thank you, Martha. I don't know what I would do without you.

Martha smiled. Well, I'm just glad to see you so happy, Seraphina. And I have a feeling that this is just the beginning of something truly special.

Seraphina nodded, feeling a sense of excitement and anticipation build within her. She knew that her and Dr. Richard's had a lot to learn about each other, but she couldn't shake the feeling that they were meant to be together.

As they continued to talk, Seraphina couldn't help but feel grateful for Martha and her matchmaking skills. She had always been there for Seraphina, offering her love and support, and now she had helped her find a love like she had never known before.

Seraphina knew that she still had a lot to learn about love and relationships, but she was willing to take the leap of faith and see where it would lead her. She knew that she and Dr. Richard's still had a lot to learn about each other, but she still couldn't shake the feeling that they were meant to be together.

Seraphina understood that love and relationships were complex and required growth and exploration. While she felt a strong connection with Dr. Richard, she recognized that both of them had much to learn about each other's intricacies. This awareness did not deter her, instead, it fueled her determination to embrace the journey ahead. She believed that taking a leap of faith was essential, as it could lead to deeper understanding and emotional intimacy.

The relationship between Seraphina and Dr. Richard was characterized by a blend of curiosity and caution. They were both aware of their past experiences and the lessons they had learned, which made them more equipped to navigate the challenges that lay ahead. Seraphina often reflected on the importance of communication and vulnerability in building a meaningful connection. This understanding motivated her to open up and share her thoughts and feelings, fostering a sense of trust between them.

Despite the uncertainties, Seraphina felt an undeniable pull towards Dr. Richard. It was as if fate had intertwined their paths, suggesting that they were meant to be together. This feeling was not just based on attraction, it was rooted in a deeper recognition of shared values and aspirations. Seraphina found comfort in the idea that their relationship could evolve into something profound, as they both sought to understand each other better.

As they spent more time together, Seraphina and Dr. Richard began to explore the nuances of their relationship. They engaged in meaningful conversations that revealed their hopes, dreams, and fears. This process of discovery was exhilarating for Seraphina, as she realized that love was not merely about romantic gestures but also about mutual respect and support. Each moment they shared brought them closer, reinforcing her belief that they were on the right path.

Ultimately, Seraphina's willingness to embrace the unknown and her commitment to personal growth set the stage for a transformative relationship with Dr. Richard. She understood that love was a journey, not a destination, and she was ready to navigate it with an open heart. This leap of faith, grounded in mutual understanding and respect, held the promise of a beautiful connection that could flourish over time.

As they finished their conversation, Seraphina hugged Martha tightly. Thank you, Martha. I don't know what I would do without you. Martha smiled back at her you will never have to find out, Seraphina. I'll always be here for you, no matter what.

Seraphina felt a sense of peace wash over her. She knew that she had found something truly special in Dr. Richard's, but she also knew that she had a strong support system in Martha. And with that, she knew she could face whatever the future held, with love, light, and hope.

As Seraphina left Martha's house, she couldn't help but feel grateful for the love and light that surrounded her. And so, with a heart full of love and light, Seraphina set off on her new journey, ready to face whatever the future held, with the warmth and support of her dear friend Martha and the love of Dr. Richard's by her side.

But as she walked down the street Seraphina couldn't shake the feeling that her journey was far from over, that there were still many twists and turns that lay ahead. But with her heart full of love and light, she was ready for whatever came her way.

As she looked up to the sky, Seraphina whispered a prayer of gratitude and love. Thank you, Martha. Thank you Dr. Richard's. And thank you God, for bringing me to this place, and for filling my heart with love and light.

And with that, Seraphina continued on her journey, her heart full of love and light, and a smile on her face, knowing she was exactly where she was meant to be.

# Chapter Twenty Two

Seraphina walked through the quiet streets, the glow of the streetlights casting a soft halo around her. The evening air was cool and crisp, a gentle breeze carrying the whispers of the night. As she neared her home, a sense of peace washed over her, wrapping her in a warm embrace.

But as Seraphina stepped onto her front porch, she heard something different, something ethereal and otherworldly. It was as if the very air around her was alive with a soft, melodious voice, echoing words of love and encouragement. At first, she thought it was just the wind playing tricks on her ears, but as she listened more closely, she realized that the whispers were coming from within her own heart.

With a trembling hand, Seraphina reached out, as if to touch the source of the echoes. In that moment, she heard a voice so pure and gentle that it brought tears to her eyes. It was the voice of God, speaking directly to her soul, assuring her that she was on the right path and that she was loved and cherished beyond measure. This divine encounter filled her with a profound sense of peace and purpose, reinforcing her faith and commitment to her spiritual journey.

Seraphina sank to her knees, overwhelmed by the emotions coursing through her. Despite the numerous hardships she had faced, including trials that tested her faith, she knew now that God was with her, guiding her every step. This realization brought a deep sense of gratitude, as she reflected on the love and support that had sustained her through the darkest times. Her heart swelled with thankfulness, and she felt a renewed sense of strength and determination to continue her path.

As she knelt there, Seraphina's mind wandered back to the challenges she had overcome. Each obstacle had seemed insurmountable at the time, yet she had persevered, driven by an unwavering belief in her divine purpose. The voice she heard now was a testament to her resilience and faith, a confirmation that her struggles were not in vain. She understood that each trial had been a stepping stone, leading her closer to this moment of divine clarity.

The voice of God resonated within her, echoing through her soul and reaffirming her mission. Seraphina realized that her journey was not just about personal salvation but also about inspiring others. Her experiences had equipped her with the wisdom and empathy needed to guide those who struggled with their own faith. She felt a calling to share her story, to be a beacon of hope for others seeking solace and direction in their lives.

With renewed vigor, Seraphina rose from her knees, ready to embrace her destiny. The voice of God had not only comforted her but also ignited a fire within her soul. She was determined to live a life that reflected the love and grace she had received, to be a living testament to the power of faith and divine guidance. As she moved forward, she carried with her the certainty that she was never alone, that she was cherished beyond measure, and that her path was divinely ordained.

As she sat there, bathed in the whispers of light and love, Seraphina knew that she was exactly where she was meant to be. And as she closed her eyes and offered up a prayer of thanks, she felt a profound sense of peace settle over her, knowing that no matter what lay ahead, she would always have God by her side.

# Chapter Twenty Three

Seraphina's heart fluttered as she heard the unexpected knock on her door. With a sense of curiosity and a touch of apprehension, she made her way to answer it, wrapping her robe tightly around her. The sound sent a rush of adrenaline through her, igniting a mix of curiosity and apprehension. She wrapped her robe tightly around herself, feeling both vulnerable and excited. As she approached the door, her mind raced with possibilities about who could be visiting her at this hour. The moment she opened the door, her breath caught in her throat at the sight of Dr. Richard standing there, a bouquet of flowers in his hands. His presence was both a surprise and a delight, leaving her momentarily speechless.

I wasn't expecting your visit, she stammered, her cheeks flushing with a blend of excitement and confusion. The unexpectedness of his arrival added to the thrill of the moment. She stepped aside to let him in, her heart racing as she invited him into her home. Please come in, Dr. Richard. Welcome to my humble abode. It's not much to the eyes, but it's my cozy home. The warmth of her invitation contrasted with the chill of the evening air, creating an intimate atmosphere that made her feel both anxious and elated.

Dr. Richard smiled warmly as he stepped inside, his expression revealing genuine gratitude for her hospitality. Thank you for inviting me in, he replied, his voice soothing her nerves. I hope I'm not intruding. I've just missed you dearly and wanted to spend the entire day with you to get to know you better. His words wrapped around her like a comforting blanket, easing her initial apprehension. The mention of Martha, who had shared her address, added a layer of familiarity to the encounter, making it feel less random and more intentional.

Dr. Richard smiled warmly, grateful for the invitation. Thank you for inviting me in, he replied. Seraphina's heart swelled with a mixture of joy and nervousness. I'm so glad you're here, she admitted softly. I thought about you all night, deep into my slumber.

As they sat together in Seraphina's quaint living room, a bittersweet feeling lingered in the air. Despite the warmth of their connection, both Seraphina and Dr. Richard carried secrets and sorrows that weighed heavily on their hearts. The day unfolded with shared laughter and moments of vulnerability, but underneath it all, a sense of impending sadness loomed.

As they settled into the cozy space, Seraphina couldn't help but notice the way Dr. Richard's eyes sparkled with enthusiasm. The flowers he brought were vibrant and fragrant, filling the room with a fresh scent that seemed to heighten the moment's significance. They began to talk, their conversation flowing effortlessly as they shared stories and laughter. Each word exchanged felt like a step closer to understanding one another, and Seraphina found herself captivated by his charm and sincerity.

As the day was unfolding like a beautiful tapestry, woven with shared experiences and budding emotions. Seraphina realized that this unexpected visit was more than just a chance encounter, it was a pivotal moment that could change the course of her life. As they continued to talk and laugh, she felt her heart flutter again, not from surprise this time, but from the blossoming connection between them. In that cozy space, surrounded by flowers and warmth, Seraphina knew that this was just the beginning of something wonderful.

Seraphina's heart swelled with a mixture of joy and nervousness. I'm so glad you're here, she admitted softly. I thought about you all night, deep into my slumber.

As they sat together in Seraphina's quaint living room, a bittersweet feeling lingered in the air. Despite the warmth of their connection, both Seraphina and Dr. Richard carried secrets and sorrows that weighed heavily on their hearts. The day unfolded with shared laughter and moments of vulnerability, but underneath it all, a sense of impending sadness loomed.

As the day drew to a close, Seraphina couldn't shake the feeling of impending goodbye that hung over them. Dr. Richard's presence was a reminder of fleeting happiness, a temporary respite from the shadows that haunted them both. And as the sun set on their time together, Seraphina knew that their fleeting moments of joy would soon be swallowed by the darkness of their own personal struggles.

With a heavy heart, Seraphina bid farewell to Dr. Richard, watching him disappear into the night. Alone once more in her cozy home, she couldn't help but feel the weight of unspoken words and unshared truths that lingered between them. And as she settled back into the quiet solitude of her space, the echoes of their brief encounter continued to haunt her, a poignant reminder of the fragile beauty of fleeting connections in a world filled with hidden sorrows.

# Chapter Twenty Four

Seraphina's heart felt heavy as she sat across from Martha, her mind swirling with conflicting emotions. The whispers of light danced across the room, casting a soft glow on their faces as she confided in her dear friend. Martha listened intently, her gaze filled with empathy and understanding.

As Seraphina recounted her day with Dr. Richard's, a sense of unease settled over her. There were moments, subtle and fleeting, where unspoken words hung heavy in the air between them. She was torn, unsure of whether to lay bare the haunting memories of her past with Lysander or to bury them deep and start anew.

The memories of Lysander were a constant presence in her life, a shadow that refused to dissipate. These memories were not just recollections of past events but reminders of the pain and hurt he had left behind. The emotional wounds inflicted by Lysander lingered, affecting her daily life and interactions. She found herself haunted by the choices he made and the consequences that followed, unable to escape the shadow of his actions. The burden of these memories weighed heavily on her, influencing her thoughts and emotions, and making it difficult to move forward.

Faced with the decision of whether to confide in Dr. Richard's, she found herself at a crossroads. Sharing her past with him could provide relief and understanding, allowing her to process and heal from the pain Lysander left behind. However, it also meant exposing herself to vulnerability and the possibility of judgment. The fear of being defined by her past and the passing of Lysander was daunting. She grappled with the notion of whether revealing her history would help her find closure or if it would only serve to deepen the scars she already bore.

On the other hand, the prospect of a fresh start was enticing. She longed to break free from the shackles of old sorrows and embrace a future untainted by past grievances. This path required courage and a willingness to let go of the past, something that was easier said than done. The idea of starting anew, unburdened by the memories of Lysander, offered a glimmer of hope. It was a chance to redefine herself and her life, to create a narrative that was her own, free from the shadows that had followed her for so long. Ultimately, the decision rested on whether she could find the strength to either confront her past or forge ahead into the unknown.

Martha's wise eyes met Seraphina's, offering solace and guidance. In that moment, Seraphina knew what she had to do. With a heavy heart and a resolve born of courage, she made a decision. It was time to confront the echoes of her past, to speak the unspoken words that had long been trapped within her.

Taking a deep breath, Seraphina steeled herself for the conversation ahead. Dr. Richard's deserved to know the truth, to understand the depths of her pain and the scars it had left behind. And so, with Martha's unwavering support, Seraphina set out to lay bare her soul, to let the whispers of light guide her on a path towards healing and forgiveness.

# Chapter Twenty Five

Seraphina stood frozen on Dr. Richard's doorstep, her heart heavy with the weight of her past and the loss of Lysander. The whispers of light that had guided her here now felt distant and cold as she realized the truth before her eyes. Two small children, with eyes so familiar, opened the door and called out Dad.

Tears welled up in Seraphina's eyes as she realized the depth of Dr. Richard's pain, the unspoken words that had passed between them on that fateful day when he had visited her home. It was a moment that transcended mere conversation, a silent exchange that spoke volumes about their shared experiences. The weight of unexpressed emotions lingered in the air, a testament to the profound connection that had formed between them. Both carried burdens of grief and longing, yet neither had fully understood the extent of the other's sorrow until that moment.

Seraphina's visit had been unexpected, yet it had brought to light the parallel paths they had walked. Each had faced personal losses that left indelible marks on their hearts. For Seraphina, the loss of a loved one had created a void filled with unending yearning. Dr. Richard, too, bore the scars of his own past, hidden beneath a veneer of professional composure. Their meeting was not just a chance encounter but a convergence of two souls seeking solace in shared understanding.

The silent understanding of grief between Seraphina and Dr. Richard was a powerful force, binding them in ways words could not. It was as if they had found a mirror in each other, reflecting back the pain and longing they had tried to suppress. This mutual recognition of suffering forged a bond that transcended the ordinary, creating a space where vulnerability was not only accepted but embraced. In each other's presence, they found a rare kind of empathy that offered comfort amidst their individual struggles.

As Seraphina stood at the front door, the room seemed to hold its breath, acknowledging the gravity of the moment. Seraphina's tears were not just an expression of her own grief but also a response to the unspoken pain she perceived in Dr. Richard. It was a cathartic release, a moment of healing that neither had anticipated. The shared sorrow became a bridge, connecting their lives in a way that was both unexpected and profound.

In the aftermath of their meeting, Seraphina and Dr. Richard carried with them a renewed sense of hope. The understanding they had found in each other was a reminder that even in the depths of despair, one is never truly alone. Their stories, though marked by loss, were also tales of resilience and the enduring power of human connection. Through their shared sorrow, they discovered a path toward healing, illuminated by the silent understanding they had forged together.

As the children embraced their father, Seraphina felt a pang of bittersweet sadness wash over her. She had come to Dr. Richard seeking solace and understanding, but instead, she had uncovered a sorrowful truth that connected them in ways she had never imagined.

With a heavy heart, Seraphina turned away from the door, leaving behind the echoes of light that now seemed dim and distant. The weight of her past and the passing of Lysander pressed down on her as she walked away, carrying with her the shared sadness of two souls bound by loss and unspoken words.

# Chapter Twenty Six

Dr. Richard's voice echoed through the air, desperation laced in every syllable as he yelled for Seraphina to stop and listen. But she continued to walk away, her steps heavy with the burden of unwavering sadness. The news of Lysander's passing had struck her to the core, leaving her heart heavy and her mind clouded with grief.

As she walked further from Dr. Richard, his own sorrow seemed distant in comparison to the depth of Seraphina's despair. He had lost a wife and the mother of his children, but Seraphina felt she had lost a piece of her soul as well. The weight of her sadness was palpable, dragging her down with each passing moment.

AS SERAPHINA WALKED further from Dr. Richard, her despair deepened, overshadowing his own sorrow. Dr. Richard had experienced a profound loss with the passing of his wife, who was also the mother of his children. However, Seraphina's grief transcended the loss of a loved one, it felt as though a part of her very essence had been torn away. This profound sense of loss weighed heavily on her, making each step more burdensome than the last. Her sadness was not just emotional but seemed to manifest physically, pulling her down with an almost tangible force.

The contrast between Dr. Richard's and Seraphina's grief highlights the different ways individuals experience and process loss. While Dr. Richard's sorrow was profound, it was rooted in the tangible loss of a partner and a mother to his children. In contrast, Seraphina's despair felt more existential, as if she had lost a part of her identity or soul. This difference in their experiences underscores the complexity of grief, which can vary greatly from person to person, influenced by the nature of the relationship and individual coping mechanisms.

Seraphina's journey through her grief is a testament to the depth of human emotion and the challenges of navigating profound loss. Her despair was not merely a response to the absence of a loved one but a reflection of a deeper, more personal void. As she distanced herself physically from Dr. Richard, she also seemed to retreat into her own world of sorrow, where the weight of her emotions was inescapable. This narrative captures the essence of how grief can be an isolating experience, drawing individuals into an introspective journey as they seek to reconcile their loss with their ongoing lives.

Despite Dr. Richard's pleas for understanding, Seraphina's footsteps never faltered. She couldn't bear to confront the reality of Lysander's absence, or the magnitude of pain Dr. Richard's and his children had experienced. It was all too much for Seraphina to bear in the moment, as Seraphina couldn't even bring herself to face the gaping hole Lysander passing had left in her life. And so, she walked away, leaving behind a trail of unspoken words and shattered emotions.

In that moment, the distance between them seemed insurmountable, a chasm of grief and misunderstanding. And as Seraphina disappeared around the corner, the silence that followed was filled with the echoes of what could have been, the words left unsaid, and the pain that lingered between them.

# Chapter Twenty Seven

Dr. Richard made his way to Seraphina's home, his heart heavy with the weight of their unfinished conversation. He had been searching for the right words to explain, to make things right between them. Seraphina opened the door, her eyes filled with sorrow and regret.

I'm sorry, Dr. Richard, she began, her voice barely above a whisper. I was overwhelmed with grief and sadness. I didn't mean to walk away without letting you explain.

Dr. Richard's heart softened at her words, understanding the pain that had led her to that moment. I know, Seraphina. I know. I have my own sadness, my own struggles. But I really like you, and I want to make things right. Can we please talk about it?

I didn't mean to walk away without letting you explain." These words marked a turning point for both Seraphina and Dr. Richard, as they navigated the complex emotions that grief often brings. Grief is a universal experience, yet it can feel isolating and overwhelming. It can manifest as intense sorrow, longing, and a preoccupation with the deceased, making it difficult for individuals to engage in everyday activities or relationships.

Dr. Richard's response to Seraphina's apology was one of understanding and empathy. He acknowledged his own struggles and expressed a desire to mend their relationship. This interaction highlights the importance of communication and support in the grieving process. Grief can often lead to misunderstandings and emotional distance, but open dialogue can help bridge these gaps. By expressing their feelings, both Seraphina and Dr. Richard took a crucial step toward healing.

Grief is not just a personal experience, it is a social one as well. The support of friends, family, and professionals can be invaluable in helping individuals navigate their emotions. This support can provide a sense of community and shared experience, which can be comforting during times of loss. Dr. Richard, likely understood the importance of providing a safe space for Seraphina to express her emotions and work through her grief.

The process of grieving is not linear, and it can vary greatly from person to person. Some may experience what is known as complicated grief, where the symptoms are more intense and prolonged. This can include difficulty accepting the loss, intense anger, or a diminished sense of self. Understanding these differences is crucial for providing appropriate support and care to those who are grieving.

Ultimately, the interaction between Seraphina and Dr. Richard underscores the healing power of empathy and understanding. By acknowledging their own emotions and those of others, individuals can begin to move through their grief in a healthy and adaptive way. This journey requires patience, compassion, and the willingness to confront and embrace the pain of loss, allowing for eventual healing and the possibility of a meaningful life beyond grief.

Seraphina hesitated, her eyes flickering with uncertainty. But then, with a nod, she stepped aside, inviting Dr. Richard into her home. And as they sat down to talk, the air between them filled with understanding and forgiveness, paving the way for a new beginning.

# Chapter Twenty Eight

Once the air had finally been cleared between Seraphina and Dr. Richards, a newfound sense of peace settled between them. They both felt they were now on safe grounds to move forward together. Dr. Richards, a man of few words, decided to open up to Seraphina one evening. He shared with her the heart wrenching story of how he lost his ex wife to stage four cancer, leaving him with their two children to raise alone.

As Dr. Richards narrated the painful chapters of his past, Seraphina found herself drawn closer to him. She could see the strength and resilience that he had exhibited in the face of such sorrow. Seraphina, too, had her own share of sad memories that lingered in her heart. However, the connection between them seemed to grow stronger as they bared their souls to each other.

Seraphina could sense the weight of his pain and the depth of his character. His ability to navigate through adversity with strength and resilience struck a chord within her, resonating with her own experiences of hardship. In those tender moments of shared vulnerability, a bond began to form between them, built on mutual understanding and empathy.

Despite the sorrowful tales that they both carried within their hearts, there was a certain beauty in the way they found solace in each other's company. Seraphina discovered a sense of kinship with Dr. Richards, recognizing that their shared experiences of pain had the power to unite them in a profound way. As they delved deeper into their pasts, the walls that had previously shielded their vulnerabilities began to crumble, allowing for a genuine connection to blossom.

In the midst of their conversation, Seraphina realized that there was a healing power in the act of opening up and sharing. Despite the shadows of their pasts, Seraphina and Dr. Richards found solace in each other's company.

They discovered a shared sense of hope that shimmered brightly in their eyes. As they held hands that evening, they knew that their path ahead might not be easy, but they were determined to walk it together, supporting each other through every challenge that came their way.

With a newfound sense of understanding and compassion, Seraphina and Dr. Richards embarked on a remarkable journey together, leaning on each other for support and guidance. The healing power of their love began to mend the wounds of their pasts, bringing solace and comfort to their hearts. They recognized the significance of letting go of the darkness that once overshadowed their lives, and instead chose to embrace the light of the future with optimism and hope.

As Seraphina and Dr. Richards delved deeper into their shared experiences and vulnerabilities, they discovered a profound connection that transcended the barriers of their individual traumas. Their willingness to be vulnerable with one another created a strong foundation for their relationship, fostering an environment of trust and understanding. Through open communication and empathy, they were able to acknowledge each other's pain and offer comfort in times of need, solidifying their bond even further.

The journey of healing and renewal that Seraphina and Dr. Richards embarked upon was not without its challenges, but Seraphina and Dr. Richards embraced the future with open hearts, leaving the darkness of their pasts behind. Together, they found the courage to heal each other's wounds, cherishing the love that bloomed between them as they embarked on a journey of healing and renewal.

# Chapter Twenty Nine

The next day, Seraphina and Dr. Richard woke up with a sense of eager anticipation as they prepared for a special gathering with their dear friends, Martha and her husband, Dan. The air was filled with excitement as they busied themselves setting up the garden for the evening's festivities. The gentle rustle of leaves and the soft chirping of birds heralded the beginning of what promised to be a memorable evening.

As they meticulously arranged fairy lights in the garden, Seraphina and Dr. Richard shared laughter and affectionate glances, their bond strengthened by the shared excitement of hosting their friends. The warm glow of the lights created a magical ambiance, turning the garden into a enchanting haven where cherished memories would be made.

Martha and Dan arrived just as the sun began to set, greeted by the sight of the beautifully decorated garden and the inviting aroma of freshly prepared food wafting through the air. Warm hugs were exchanged, and joyful laughter filled the air as they settled into their environment.

As dusk settled in, the friends gathered around a crackling fire pit, sharing stories and laughter. Seraphina and Martha reminisced about their college days, while Dr. Richard and Dan discussed their shared love for hiking and nature.

The night was filled with lively conversations, delicious food, and the warmth of friendship. Under the starlit sky, they toasted to many more gatherings like this one, cherishing the bond they shared.

As the night grew late, they bid each other farewell, promising to meet again soon. Seraphina and Dr. Richard watched their friends drive off, feeling grateful for the wonderful evening spent in the company of loved ones. It was a night to remember, a reminder of the joy that friendship brings.

Seraphina and Martha eagerly devised a new plan to bring Dr. Richard, and Dan together the following day with a shared mission of spreading light throughout the town of Lottersville. Enthusiasm filled the room as they discussed how they could collectively make a positive impact on their community. Seraphina, with her creative ideas, proposed setting up a series of small events and activities throughout the town to brighten people's days and promote unity among neighbors. Martha, being the charismatic leader she was, took charge of organizing the logistics and rallying support from local businesses and volunteers.

The next day, as the sun rose over Lottersville, Seraphina, Martha, Dr. Richard, and Dan joined forces to kick off their day of spreading light. They embarked on a journey of kindness, starting with uplifting messages scattered around the town, followed by random acts of generosity towards strangers they encountered. Their efforts not only brought smiles to people's faces but also sparked a sense of community spirit that resonated throughout Lottersville. By the end of the day, the quartet had succeeded in brightening the town with their love, compassion, and dedication to making a difference.

# Chapter Thirty

Seraphina and Dr. Richard had been secretly planning their future together for months. Their love blossomed as they spent time getting to know each other over long walks in the park, cozy dinners, and shared laughter. They both knew that they wanted to spend the rest of their lives together, but there was one thing missing to make their family complete an addition that would fill their lives with even more joy and laughter.

One crisp autumn day, Seraphina felt a flutter of happiness deep within her as she discovered that she was expecting a baby with Dr. Richard. The news filled her heart with joy and brought a radiant smile to her face. Seraphina had always dreamed of becoming a mother, and now that dream was finally coming true. She couldn't contain her excitement and felt an overwhelming sense of gratitude for the new life growing inside her.

As the sun cast a golden hue over the changing leaves, Seraphina couldn't wait to share the incredible news with her best friends, Martha and Dan. They were more than just friends to her; they were like family. The four of them had forged a bond that went beyond mere companionship, having stood by each other through thick and thin. Seraphina knew that Martha and Dan would be overjoyed to hear about her pregnancy and would offer their unwavering support every step of the way.

When Seraphina finally gathered her friends together to share her news, their faces lit up with happiness and surprise. Martha enveloped Seraphina in a warm hug, tears of joy glistening in her eyes. Dan congratulated Dr. Richard with a hearty handshake, his eyes shining with delight. The room was filled with an air of celebration and love as they toasted to the new life that was blooming within Seraphina, the anticipation and excitement palpable in the air.

As the days turned into weeks, Seraphina's bond with Martha and Dan grew even stronger. They accompanied her to doctor's appointments, listened to her pregnancy cravings and woes, and showered her with love and support. The impending arrival of the baby brought them even closer together, sharing in the anticipation and wonder of this new chapter in Seraphina's life. Together, they laughed, cried, and cherished each moment as they awaited the arrival of the little one who would further unite their hearts.

With each passing day, Seraphina's belly grew rounder, and the excitement and anticipation mounted. Martha and Dan helped Seraphina prepare the nursery, pick out baby clothes, and plan for the future. They reveled in discussing potential names for the baby, envisioning the joy and laughter that would soon fill their lives. Seraphina felt grateful and blessed to have such incredible friends by her side, their unwavering support and friendship providing her strength and comfort during this transformative time.

As the autumn days grew cooler and the trees shed their golden leaves, Seraphina's heart swelled with love and gratitude. She knew that the journey ahead would be filled with challenges and joys, but she felt confident knowing that she had Martha and Dan by her side. The bond they shared was unbreakable, a testament to the enduring power of friendship and love. Seraphina looked forward to the future with hope and excitement, knowing that with the love of her friends and the growing family she was building, she was ready to embrace whatever lay ahead with grace and strength.

Seraphina arranged a cozy get together at their favorite cafe, where she and Dr. Richard shared the wonderful news of their pregnancy. Martha and Dan were thrilled beyond words, they couldn't contain their happiness for the couple. The table was filled with laughter, hugs, and happy tears as they toasted to the new chapter in Seraphina and Dr. Richard's life.

As the evening went on, Seraphina shared the exciting news that she would soon be moving into Dr. Richard's home to start their new family together. The couple planned to make the house a warm and welcoming place for their new baby and Dr. Richard's children from his previous marriage.

Martha and Dan couldn't be happier for their friends. They knew that Seraphina and Dr. Richard would make a wonderful family together, filled with love, laughter, and endless adventures. The group spent the evening dreaming about the future, imagining the joyful chaos that would soon fill Dr. Richard's home.

And so, with hearts full of happiness and anticipation, Seraphina and Dr. Richard embarked on this new journey together, supported by their dear friends, Martha and Dan, who would always be there to share in their joys and support them in moments of need.

# Chapter Thirty One

Dr. Richard, a well known pediatrician, was blessed with two wonderful children, Lucas and Amy. Lucas was a curious little boy with a heart of gold, while Amy was a bright and cheerful girl always ready for an adventure.

Seraphina had a gentle smile and a warm presence that instantly captured the hearts of Lucas and Amy.

As days turned into weeks, Seraphina formed a special bond with the children. She spent time playing with them, reading stories, and helping them with their homework. Lucas and Amy adored Seraphina and looked forward to her visits to their home.

One day, Seraphina shared the wonderful news that she was expecting a baby. Lucas and Amy were overjoyed at the thought of a new addition to their family. They showered Seraphina with love and affection, talking excitedly about becoming older siblings.

Filled with happiness, Lucas and Amy approached Seraphina one evening, their eyes sparkling with anticipation. Can we call you mother? they asked, their voices eager and hopeful.

Touched by their heartfelt request, Seraphina smiled warmly. Of course you can, she replied, her heart swelling with love. It would be my honor to be your mother, and I can't wait for the next chapter of our lives together.

The news of Seraphina's pregnancy spread like sunshine through a garden of flowers, illuminating the hearts of those around her. Lucas and Amy, her two beloved children, were particularly affected by the announcement. They had always dreamed of having a sibling to play with, to share their secrets, and to grow alongside. As they hugged Seraphina tightly, their laughter filled the room, it was a sound of pure joy, a melody that danced around the walls and settled into every corner of their home. The prospect of becoming older siblings brought a new energy into their lives, one that promised adventure and love.

As days turned into weeks, the anticipation grew. Lucas and Amy began to imagine what life would be like with a new baby in the house. They envisioned themselves teaching the little one how to ride a bike, helping with homework, and sharing their favorite toys. The thought of bedtime stories, family game nights, and all the laughter that lay ahead made their hearts flutter with excitement. Every day, they would ask Seraphina about the baby, What will their name be? Will they have curly hair like me? The questions poured out of them like a waterfall, each one more curious than the last.

Seraphina reveled in their excitement, appreciating how deeply they embraced the idea of a new family member. Every time she answered their questions, she felt a bond strengthening between them. She began to imagine the little hands that would wrap around her fingers, the soft coos and giggles that would fill their home, and the countless memories they would create together. Seraphina knew that this journey wouldn't just be about her and the new baby; it was about the entire family coming together to nurture and support one another.

It was a moment that encapsulated the essence of family love, acceptance, and a shared journey. The word 'mother had never felt so right, so full of promise. In that instant, Seraphina knew that she was not only welcoming a new child into the world, but she was also affirming the love that already existed within her family.

As the days passed, the reality of their new dynamic began to take shape. Lucas and Amy took it upon themselves to help prepare for the baby's arrival. They carefully selected items from their toys to donate, clearing space for the new addition. They painted the nursery with vibrant colors, their creativity spilling out onto the walls. Each brushstroke was filled with their hopes and dreams for their sibling, and they felt proud knowing they were contributing to this new life.

Seraphina watched with immense pride as her children poured their hearts into every task. She marveled at their kindness and generosity, qualities that would surely make them wonderful older siblings. The more they engaged in the preparations, the more their anticipation grew, and it was infectious. Soon, the entire household buzzed with excitement, and Seraphina found herself daydreaming about the family traditions they would create together, the lessons they would learn, and the love they would share.

And so, in that moment, a new family was formed, bound not only by blood but by love, respect, and mutual adoration. Dr. Richard watched with pride as his children embraced Seraphina as their mother, knowing that their home would forever be filled with laughter, warmth, and the beautiful bond of a family united in love.

# Chapter Thirty Two

In the town of Lottersville, known for its charming countryside, beautiful wildflowers, and brightly colored row houses, a joyous occasion was about to take place. The townspeople known for their welcoming, were buzzing with excitement as they went about their daily routines. Little did they know that today Dr. Richard would ask for Seraphina hand in marriage. The beautiful woman who had captured his heart.

Lottersville, where the rolling hills met the horizon and wildflowers painted the fields with vibrant hues, a sense of anticipation hung in the air. The townsfolk, known for their warm smiles and open hearts, moved through their daily routines with a lively energy that hinted at the special event scheduled for that day. Children laughed as they played in the sun drenched streets, while shopkeepers exchanged friendly banter with their customers. The charm of the brightly colored row houses added to the vibrant atmosphere, creating a feeling of community that enveloped everyone in its embrace.

As the sun rose higher in the sky, casting golden rays upon the town, Dr. Richard felt a mix of excitement and nervousness fluttering in his chest. He had long admired Seraphina, the beautiful woman who had effortlessly captured his heart. Her laughter was like music to his ears, and her kindness resonated with everyone around her. Today was the day he had chosen to take a leap of faith and ask for her hand in marriage. He envisioned a future filled with love, laughter, and shared dreams, but first, he needed to summon the courage to express his feelings.

In the heart of Lottersville, the town square bustled with activity. Vendors displayed their fresh produce, artisans showcased their handmade crafts, and the air was filled with the aroma of baked goods wafting from the local bakery. Dr. Richard took a moment to absorb the beauty of it all, knowing that he wanted to create a life with Seraphina that mirrored the charm and warmth of their beloved town. He had meticulously planned a small gathering in the square, inviting friends and family to witness his proposal, hoping it would be a joyous occasion that would forever be etched in their memories.

As the clock struck noon, the town square began to fill with familiar faces. Laughter and chatter enveloped the air while colorful banners swayed gently in the breeze, creating a festive atmosphere. Dr. Richard's heart raced as he glanced at Seraphina, who was radiant in a flowing sundress embellished with wildflowers. Her beauty was captivating, and he felt a surge of love and admiration. He knew this was the moment he had been waiting for, and he couldn't let it pass him by.

Gathering his friends and family around, Dr. Richard took a deep breath and stepped forward, his voice steady but filled with emotion. Thank you all for coming together today, he began, his gaze fixed on Seraphina. Each of you has played a vital role in my life, and today, I want to share something special. The crowd hushed, the excitement palpable as they sensed the significance of his words. Seraphina's eyes sparkled with curiosity, her heart racing as she wondered what he had planned.

With a flourish, Dr. Richard reached into his pocket and retrieved a small, velvet box. The crowd gasped softly, and Seraphina's breath caught in her throat. He knelt before her, the world around them fading into a blur as he focused solely on her. Seraphina, he said, his voice unwavering, "from the moment I met you, my life changed in ways I never thought possible. You are my confidante, my joy, and my greatest blessing. Will you make me the happiest man in Lottersville and marry me?"

Tears of happiness filled Seraphina's eyes as she looked at the man she adored. It was as if time stood still, the vibrant colors of the town swirling around them in a beautiful dance. The crowd erupted into cheers and applause, their joy echoing through the square. Seraphina's heart swelled with love, and she nodded, her voice filled with emotion as she replied, Yes! Yes, I will marry you! The moment was magical, a celebration of love that would resonate in the hearts of all who witnessed it.

As Dr. Richard slipped the ring onto her finger, the townspeople erupted into joyous laughter and applause. Flower petals rained down from above, tossed by delighted children who had been eagerly waiting for this moment.

In that instant, Lottersville felt even more enchanting, as if the very essence of love had woven itself into the fabric of the town. Dr. Richard and Seraphina embraced, their hearts beating as one, while friends and family surrounded them with cheers of congratulations.

In the days that followed, the town of Lottersville buzzed with excitement as preparations for the wedding began. The couple worked tirelessly to create a celebration that reflected their love and the beauty of their surroundings. The vibrant wildflowers that adorned the countryside would feature prominently in their decorations, and the brightly colored row houses would serve as a backdrop for the ceremony. It was a time of joy, laughter, and community spirit, as everyone came together to support the couple in their journey toward marriage.

# Chapter Thirty Three

Seraphina stood nervously at the door of Dr. Richard's grand Victorian home, her heart racing with a mix of excitement and apprehension. The ornate architecture loomed above her, its intricate details telling stories of the past while promising a bright future. She gently caressed her swollen belly, feeling the gentle kicks of her unborn child, a reminder of the new life growing within her. Today marked a significant milestone in her journey, as she prepared to move into a home that would no longer just belong to Dr. Richard, but also to her and the children they would raise together.

The grandeur of the Victorian home was overwhelming in its beauty. With its tall windows and vibrant colors, it stood as a testament to the love that had been nurtured within its walls. Seraphina took a deep breath, steeling herself for the changes that lay ahead. She had spent many evenings imagining what it would be like to live with Dr. Richard and his two children, Lucas and Amy. The thought of becoming a mother figure to them filled her with both joy and anxiety, as she wanted to ensure that she built a strong bond with them right from the start.

As she finally gathered the courage to knock, the door swung open to reveal Dr. Richard, his warm smile instantly easing some of her nerves. His eyes sparkled with affection as he took in her presence, and he stepped aside to welcome her into the home. Welcome home, Seraphina, he said softly, his voice wrapped in warmth. The words enveloped her like a comforting embrace, and she felt a sense of belonging wash over her, even amidst the uncertainty that loomed ahead.

Lucas and Amy appeared in the hallway, their faces lighting up with excitement at the sight of Seraphina. They rushed forward, eager to greet her with open arms. Seraphina! You're here! Lucas exclaimed, his enthusiasm contagious. Amy chimed in, We've been waiting for you! The children's exuberance melted away the last remnants of Seraphina's apprehension. She crouched down to meet them at eye level, her heart swelling with love. I'm so happy to be here, she replied, her voice filled with sincerity.

The initial moments in the house felt like a whirlwind of emotions. Dr. Richard guided her through the home, showing her the cozy living room adorned with family photos and the kitchen that smelled of freshly baked cookies a favorite treat of the children. Each room seemed to echo with laughter and memories, and Seraphina was eager to add her own to the tapestry of their lives. The thought of creating new traditions with Lucas and Amy filled her with anticipation, and she could already envision game nights, family dinners, and storytime routines.

As the evening approached, the family gathered in the kitchen, where Dr. Richard had prepared a simple yet delicious meal. Seraphina felt a sense of warmth enveloping her as they all sat around the table together. She glanced at the children, who were animatedly discussing their day, and she couldn't help but smile. This was the family she had always wanted, and she was finally a part of it. The laughter shared over dinner created an atmosphere of comfort, and Seraphina felt her heart expand with each moment.

After dinner, Dr. Richard suggested a movie night, and the children cheered in delight. They all settled into the living room, blankets draped over their laps as they prepared to watch a beloved family film. Seraphina nestled close to Dr. Richard, feeling the warmth of his presence beside her. As the movie played, she occasionally glanced at Lucas and Amy, who were engrossed in the story unfolding on the screen. In those moments, she felt a profound sense of gratitude for this new chapter of her life.

As the credits rolled, the children clamored for a bedtime story, and Seraphina eagerly jumped at the opportunity. She had always dreamed of being a storyteller, and now she had the chance to share her love for stories with Lucas and Amy. Together, they retreated to the cozy nook in their home, where Seraphina read aloud, her voice weaving tales of adventure and wonder. The children listened intently, their eyes wide with imagination, and Seraphina felt a deep connection forming with them.

That night, as Seraphina lay in bed beside Dr. Richard, she reflected on the whirlwind of emotions that had transpired throughout the day. She felt a sense of peace settling in her heart, knowing that they were all embarking on this journey together. The love she felt for Dr. Richard deepened with each passing moment, and she couldn't help but smile at the thought of the family they would build. Tomorrow would bring new challenges, but together, they would create a life filled with love, laughter, and cherished memories.

As she closed her eyes, Seraphina whispered a silent prayer of gratitude for the beautiful family she had been blessed with.

# Chapter Thirty Four

Seraphina finally found solace in Dr. Richard's home, where she had settled into a new rhythm of life with their two children, Lucas and Amy. The warmth of the Victorian house enveloped her like a soft embrace, and she felt a sense of belonging that had eluded her for so long. As her pregnancy progressed smoothly, a gentle glow radiated from her, reflecting the joy and anticipation that filled their household. Each day seemed to bring new milestones, and the thought of expanding their family filled her with hope and excitement.

Over time, Seraphina had grown to adore Lucas and Amy, embracing them as her own. The initial nervousness she had felt upon moving in had melted away, replaced by a deep affection for the children who had quickly become an integral part of her life. They shared moments of laughter and play, creating a bond that felt unbreakable. Whether it was building forts with cushions or embarking on imaginative adventures in their backyard, their days were filled with joy, and Seraphina cherished every second spent with them.

One of Seraphina's favorite pastimes was teaching Amy how to sew. She had mastered this skill over the years, finding solace in the rhythmic motion of needle and thread. As they sat together in the cozy corner of the living room, surrounded by colorful fabrics and patterns, Seraphina felt a sense of fulfillment. Guiding Amy through the intricate art of stitching was not just about teaching a skill, it was about sharing a piece of herself and creating lasting memories together.

Now, remember, Amy, Seraphina said, her voice gentle yet encouraging, the key to sewing is patience and practice. Each stitch is a step toward creating something beautiful. Amy nodded eagerly, her eyes sparkling with enthusiasm as she clutched her fabric and needle. Seraphina watched with pride as the little girl focused intently on her work, her small fingers deftly maneuvering the needle through the fabric. In those moments, Seraphina felt a deep sense of connection not only with Amy but also with the legacy of creativity she hoped to pass down.

As they stitched together, they shared stories and laughter, creating an atmosphere filled with warmth. Seraphina would recount tales from her childhood how she had learned to sew from her grandmother, who had taught her the importance of craftsmanship and creativity. Amy listened intently, fascinated by the stories of the past, and she often asked questions that made Seraphina smile. It was a beautiful exchange, one that solidified their bond and allowed Amy to see Seraphina not just as a stepmother, but as a mentor and friend.

Lucas, always intrigued by the activity, would often peek over the back of the couch, curious about what they were creating. Can I help too?he would ask, his voice full of eagerness. Seraphina would chuckle, inviting him to join in the fun. Soon, the three of them would be gathered around the table, fabrics spread out like a colorful tapestry, each one contributing their own creativity to a shared project. The laughter and chatter that filled the room became the soundtrack of their lives, a melody of familial love and connection.

One afternoon, as they worked on a patchwork quilt for the baby, Seraphina demonstrated how to sew a straight line. It's all about finding your rhythm, she explained, guiding Amy's hands as she carefully followed the seam. Just like in life, sometimes we need to adjust our course, but we always keep moving forward. Amy nodded, absorbing the wisdom hidden within the lesson. This moment was about more than just sewing, it was a life lesson wrapped in fabric and thread.

As the days turned into weeks, the quilt began to take shape, each patch telling a story of the family they were creating. Seraphina found joy in seeing Amy's confidence grow with each completed square. The little girl's excitement was infectious, and she would often clap her hands in delight when she finished a new section. This shared project became a symbol of their blossoming relationship, a tangible representation of the love they were weaving together.

Dr. Richard would often peek in on their sewing sessions, a proud smile gracing his face as he watched his fiance even and children bond over their shared creativity. He admired how Seraphina had seamlessly integrated into their lives, fostering a sense of unity and love that had been missing before.

It warmed his heart to see them laughing together, the sounds of joy echoing through the halls of their home.

As the quilt neared completion, Seraphina realized that it was not just a blanket meant for warmth, it was a reflection of their family each patch representing a shared experience, a moment of laughter, and a lesson learned. It served as a reminder that they were all connected, that together they could create something beautiful amidst the challenges life presented.

# Chapter Thirty Five

Seraphina's heart raced as she felt a sudden warmth and a rush of fluid beneath her. Her water had just broken. Panic and excitement mingled in her chest as she quickly grabbed her phone, dialing Martha's number with trembling fingers. Martha! It's happening! I'm about to deliver! Her voice was urgent, filled with a mix of joy and fear. Martha's calm voice on the other end reassured her, instructing her to breathe and assuring her that everything would be alright. Seraphina took a deep breath, feeling the adrenaline course through her veins, heightening her senses.

As she hung up the phone, the reality of the moment sank in. She was about to become a mother, a journey she had anticipated with both eagerness and trepidation. As an earth angel, Seraphina marveled at the intricate way God wove His plans into the lives of those around her. She had always felt a connection to the divine, a sense that she was part of something greater. It was as if God had orchestrated this moment, and all she had to do was pause and listen to the gentle nudges of her heart guiding her forward.

Richard! she called out, urgency lacing her voice. Dr. Richard emerged from the study, his expression shifting from surprise to understanding as he saw the frantic look in her eyes. It's time, she said, her voice trembling slightly. Without a moment's hesitation, he grabbed their hospital bag, which they had packed in anticipation of this day, and together they rushed out of their Victorian home. The warmth of their loving household was a stark contrast to the whirlwind of emotions that awaited them.

The drive to the hospital was a blur of lights and sounds, the world outside the car window flashing by in a dizzying array of colors. Seraphina could feel the contractions intensifying, each wave of pain a reminder of the life that was about to enter the world. She squeezed Dr. Richard's hand tightly, seeking comfort in his presence as he drove with purpose, his focus unwavering. In that moment, she felt the presence of divine guidance surrounding her, wrapping her in a cocoon of comfort and strength.

As they arrived at the hospital, Seraphina's heart raced with a mixture of excitement and apprehension. The sterile environment was a stark contrast to the warmth of their home, but the bright lights and bustling staff filled her with hope. She could hear the distant cries of newborns and the soft murmur of nurses attending to mothers. It was a symphony of life, a reminder of the miracle that was about to unfold.

Navigating through the chaos of the emergency room, Seraphina felt each contraction wash over her like a tide. The labor pains intensified, each wave of agony followed by a surge of anticipation and hope. She was acutely aware of the miracle of life that was unfolding within her, a life that would soon step into the world, bringing with it a new chapter of love and joy. With every breath, she focused on the beauty of creation, allowing herself to be present in the moment.

As they settled into the delivery room, Seraphina felt a mix of vulnerability and strength. The medical staff moved around her with practiced efficiency, asking questions and preparing for the birth. Richard held her hand, his presence a steady anchor amidst the whirlwind of emotions. You're doing amazing, Seraphina, he whispered, his voice soothing her frayed nerves. She looked into his eyes, finding reassurance in his unwavering support.

In between contractions, Seraphina closed her eyes and envisioned the life that awaited her. She could see herself cradling the tiny bundle in her arms, feeling the warmth of her baby's body against her skin. She thought of Lucas and Amy, who would soon have a little sibling to love and cherish. The thought filled her with an overwhelming sense of joy, a reminder that this moment was just the beginning of their beautiful family story.

As the pain surged, Seraphina surrendered to the process, allowing herself to be carried by the waves of labor. She visualized each contraction as a step closer to meeting her child. You can do this, she told herself, drawing strength from the countless women who had experienced this before her. With each breath, she felt a deep connection to the generations of mothers who had walked this path, their spirits surrounding her in support.

Finally, after what felt like an eternity, the doctor entered the room with a calm demeanor. Alright, Seraphina, it's time to bring your baby into the world, he said, his voice filled with encouragement. The moment felt monumental, and Seraphina focused on the rhythm of her breathing, channeling all her energy into the final push. Richard was right beside her, whispering words of love and encouragement, reminding her of the beautiful life they were about to welcome.

# Chapter Thirty Six

Seraphina was overjoyed as she cradled her newborn son, Noah, in her arms, feeling the weight of his tiny body against her chest. The delicate rise and fall of his breath filled her with an indescribable warmth, and she couldn't help but smile at the miracle she had brought into the world. Yet, as she prepared for the journey back home to her extended family, a cloud of sadness lingered over her like an unwelcome shadow. Despite the overwhelming happiness of welcoming Noah, a nagging emptiness crept into her heart, reminding her that not all was as it seemed.

As the car ride unfolded, the chatter of family members around her was a stark contrast to the turmoil within. Laughter and excitement filled the air, but Seraphina found it hard to engage fully. She looked out the window, watching the world blur by, her mind a jumble of thoughts. The joy of motherhood should have been enough to drown out the sadness, yet it persisted like a ghost, haunting her with reminders of the challenges that lay ahead.

Upon arriving home, the familiar surroundings that once brought her comfort felt different, almost suffocating. The walls of her Victorian house, filled with memories of love and laughter, now seemed to close in on her, amplifying the weight of her emotions. As she settled back into her routine, the heaviness grew, threatening to engulf her completely. She found herself wondering if anyone could see the storm brewing beneath her surface, if anyone could understand the battle she was fighting within.

Recognizing the signs of postpartum depression, Seraphina knew she needed help. It was a brave admission, one she had to confront head-on. She reached out to her doctor, her voice shaky but resolute as she explained her feelings. The reassurance that her emotions were normal during such a tumultuous time offered some relief, but the darkness still loomed like a dark cloud overhead. She realized that acknowledging her struggle was the first step toward healing, but it felt daunting.

With a prescription in hand, Seraphina resolved to take her journey one day at a time. Each morning, she would wake up and remind herself to cling to the hope that one day the shadows would lift, allowing her to embrace the joy of motherhood fully. Some days were easier than others; there were moments of clarity when she could see the beauty in her new role, and then there were days when the weight of sadness felt insurmountable.

Throughout this process, she leaned on the support of her family, each member stepping in to help in their own way. Richard was a steady presence, offering encouragement and understanding when the darkness threatened to pull her under. Lucas and Amy, with their innocent excitement for their new brother, brought moments of light that pierced through her heaviness, reminding her of the love that surrounded her.

Lucas and Amy could hardly contain their excitement as they welcomed their new baby brother, Noah, into the world. Each of them took turns cradling the tiny bundle of joy, their hearts swelling with love and pride. They marveled at his delicate features the way his tiny mouth opened in a soft yawn, or how he instinctively curled his tiny fingers around theirs. It was a joyous scene, filled with laughter and wonder, and for a fleeting moment, Seraphina felt her heart lift.

In that moment, the bond of siblinghood deepened. Lucas and Amy were already envisioning the adventures and laughter that awaited them as a family of five. They played imaginary games, pretending to be superheroes or explorers, with Noah as their sidekick. Their home felt warmer and more vibrant, filled with the sweet sounds of newborn coos and the gentle rustle of blankets being adjusted as they took turns ensuring Noah was comfortable and safe.

Seraphina, the earth angel, watched over her family with a heart full of gratitude and joy. Despite the shadows that lingered, she felt an overwhelming sense of purpose, knowing that this was the family and the life that God had intended for her all along. She gazed at her children, and in their laughter, she found snippets of hope glimpses of their futures filled with love, challenges, and the growth that would come from their shared experiences.

She knew that Noah was not just a new addition, he was a precious gift that would bring them closer together, weaving their lives into an even more beautiful tapestry of love and unity. In those serene moments, she whispered a silent prayer of thanks, embracing the joy of their completed family. Each day, she vowed to herself that she would not only be present for her children but also for herself, seeking the joy that felt just out of reach.

As the days turned into weeks, Seraphina began to find small pockets of happiness amidst the challenges. The first time she heard Noah giggle in his sleep, a smile broke through her sadness, warming her heart.

# Chapter Thirty Seven

In the lovely town of Lottersville, a vibrant and close knit community gathered to celebrate the arrival of a new bundle of joy. Seraphina, known far and wide for her kindness, generosity, and the light she spread through the town, had welcomed a precious baby into her family. The news of her child's birth echoed through the streets, igniting a wave of excitement among the townsfolk. Each person felt a personal connection to Seraphina, as if her happiness was intricately woven into the fabric of their own lives.

The townspeople had felt touched by Seraphina's constant acts of kindness and love that brightened their days. From helping the elderly with their groceries to organizing charity events, and sewing clothes for her community in need, Seraphina had always gone above and beyond to make everyone feel welcomed and cared for. She was a beacon of hope, a reminder of the goodness that exists in the world. Her selflessness inspired others to lend a helping hand, creating a ripple effect of compassion throughout Lottersville.

Determined to repay her for all the joy she brought into their lives, the residents of Lottersville secretly planned a surprise party to welcome Seraphina's new little one. It was a labor of love, with each person contributing their unique talents and resources. Local bakers whipped up delicious treats, artists painted vibrant banners, and musicians prepared to fill the air with lively tunes. The town square transformed into a festive wonderland, adorned with colorful decorations that reflected the spirit of love and community.

As Seraphina and her family made their way to the town square, they were met with cheers and applause from the crowd. The sound of laughter and music enveloped them, creating an atmosphere of pure joy. Seraphina's heart swelled as she took in the sight of her friends and neighbors, all gathered to celebrate.

Her eyes filled with tears of joy as she saw the outpouring of love and support from her community, a testament to the bonds they had forged over the years.

The townspeople presented her with thoughtful gifts for the baby hand knitted blankets, handmade toys, and heartfelt notes filled with wishes for a happy life. Each gift was a symbol of the care and affection that the residents of Lottersville held for Seraphina. As she accepted these tokens of love, her heart felt as though it might burst with gratitude. The moment was a poignant reminder that she was never alone; her community stood beside her, ready to support her in every way.

Amid laughter, music, and the sound of children playing, Seraphina felt overwhelmed with happiness and gratitude. She watched as her children played with their friends, their faces alight with joy, and she couldn't help but smile. It warmed her heart to see how her little ones were embraced by the same community that had nurtured her. In that moment, she realized that the true wealth of a community lies in the bonds of love and support that tie its residents together.

The party continued late into the night, with everyone dancing, singing, and celebrating the newest member of Lottersville. Seraphina held her baby close, feeling blessed to be surrounded by such a wonderful community that had come together to celebrate life, love, and the joy of new beginnings. The warmth of their affection enveloped her like a cozy blanket, and she felt an overwhelming sense of belonging.

As the evening wore on, Seraphina took a moment to step back and observe the festivities. She saw the joy on the faces of her friends, the laughter shared between neighbors, and the children playing games in the grass. It was a scene of pure happiness, one that she would cherish forever. In that moment, she felt a profound connection to each person in the crowd, realizing that their lives were intertwined in a beautiful tapestry of shared moments and memories.

Throughout the night, stories were exchanged, and laughter echoed through the square. Seraphina joined in the festivities, dancing with her children and savoring every moment. She felt the burdens of the past few weeks lift as she immersed herself in the joy surrounding her. The worries that had plagued her during her pregnancy seemed to fade into the background, replaced by the warmth of love and community.

As the sun began to set, casting a golden glow over Lottersville, the townspeople gathered for a group photo. Seraphina stood at the center, cradling her baby, surrounded by friends, family, and neighbors who had come to celebrate. The camera clicked, capturing the essence of that magical day a snapshot of love, unity, and the joy of new beginnings.

As the night drew to a close, Seraphina was filled with gratitude for the life she had built in Lottersville. The celebration had shown her that the light and love she had shared with others had come back to her a hundredfold. She looked around, seeing the faces of those who had supported her.

# Chapter Thirty Eight

Seraphina was grateful to have met Martha in the small town of Lottersville. Their friendship blossomed unexpectedly one sunny afternoon at the local farmers' market. Seraphina had been browsing the stalls, admiring the fresh produce and homemade goods, when she overheard Martha enthusiastically discussing her latest baking experiment with a vendor. The infectious laughter that followed drew Seraphina in, and before long, they were exchanging stories about their lives, dreams, and favorite recipes.

They clicked instantly, sharing not just words but a deep understanding of one another. Martha's vibrant spirit complemented Seraphina's gentle nature, creating a friendship that felt as comfortable as an old sweater. Their conversations flowed effortlessly, filled with laughter and the occasional shared sigh, creating an unbreakable bond. From that day forward, they became inseparable, two souls navigating the joys and challenges of life hand in hand.

Over the years, their bond grew stronger, woven together by countless shared experiences. They spent countless afternoons in coffee shops, sipping warm beverages while discussing everything from life's little joys to their deepest fears. They attended community events together, volunteering their time and energy to help those in need, solidifying their roles as pillars of the Lottersville community. With each passing year, their friendship deepened, becoming a source of strength and comfort for both of them.

As Seraphina looked at her life now, surrounded by love and friendship, she couldn't help but reminisce about her past. The memory of Lysander, her lost love, still lingered in her heart like a soft melody playing in the background. They had shared a beautiful love story one filled with laughter, dreams, and passion. Yet, the abrupt end of their time together had left an indelible mark on her soul.

The pain of losing Lysander was once deep and overwhelming, a void that felt insurmountable. She could still vividly recall the moments they had spent together the way he would hold her close, whispering sweet nothings that made her heart flutter. But time, as it often does, had a way of healing wounds, and the sharp edges of her grief had softened. It had become a gentle ache, a bittersweet reminder of the love they shared.

Through Martha's friendship and unwavering support, Seraphina learned that the pain of losing a loved one never truly fades away. Instead, it transforms into a soft whisper of memories that accompany us through life's journey. Together, they explored the depths of their emotions, sharing stories of love and loss, each tale a thread that connected them even more deeply. Martha's presence allowed Seraphina to confront her grief without fear, offering a safe space for her to express her feelings.

Martha would often say, Our loved ones may leave us, but their love remains a part of who we are. These words resonated within Seraphina, reminding her that while Lysander was no longer physically present, his essence continued to shape her life. She found solace in the idea that love transcends time and space, that it becomes a guiding force, steering her through the challenges of life.

With Martha by her side, Seraphina found comfort in the shared understanding of grief. They would often reminisce about the people they had lost, sharing stories that both honored their memories and allowed them to heal. There were days when laughter would erupt between them, a beautiful contrast to the tears that sometimes flowed. Those moments of joy were vital, serving as a reminder that life continues, even in the face of loss.

Seraphina discovered that it was okay to feel both sadness and joy simultaneously. It was part of the human experience, an intricate dance of emotions that defined their journey. Martha taught her that grief could coexist with happiness, that it was possible to honor the past while embracing the present. Together, they created a safe haven where they could explore their feelings without judgment, forging a deeper connection through vulnerability.

As the seasons changed in Lottersville, so did Seraphina's outlook on life. The community's vibrant celebrations became a backdrop for her healing journey, each event a reminder of the beauty that existed alongside her pain. With Martha's encouragement, she began to participate more actively, engaging in activities that brought her joy. Whether it was baking for the local charity bake sale or organizing community clean ups, each endeavor allowed her to channel her energy into something positive.

The bond between Seraphina and Martha was not just built on shared experiences, but also on mutual growth. They inspired each other to pursue their dreams, no matter how big or small. Seraphina often found herself dreaming again, envisioning a future filled with possibilities. She began sketching her aspirations, whether it was starting a community garden or writing a book about her experiences. With Martha cheering her on, she found the courage to take steps toward those dreams.

# Chapter Thirty Nine

Seraphina sat down in her favorite spot by the window, a cup of hot tea in her hands, and let her mind wander back through the years. The steam curled up from the cup, lifting her thoughts into a gentle reverie. It seemed like just yesterday that she had first met Dr. Richard, a chance encounter that had changed the course of her life forever. They had been at a community event, mingling among friends and neighbors, when their eyes met across the crowded room. The spark was immediate, electric, and she had felt a pull toward him that she couldn't quite explain.

From that moment on, their love had blossomed and grown stronger with each passing day. It was a whirlwind romance filled with laughter, late-night conversations, and shared dreams. They would spend hours discussing their hopes for the future, painting vivid pictures of the lives they wanted to build together. It was during those early days that Seraphina realized she had found her partner, someone who not only understood her but also challenged her to be her best self.

As she watched her three children playing in the yard, their laughter echoing through the house, Seraphina couldn't help but feel a sense of overwhelming gratitude. The sight of their joy, their carefree spirits running through the grass, filled her heart with warmth. She cherished these moments, knowing that they were the result of the love she and Richard had nurtured over the years. They had created a safe haven for their children, a place where they could explore, learn, and grow.

Life had its challenges, no doubt, but they had faced them all head on, together as a family. From sleepless nights with a newborn to the chaos of school projects and extracurricular activities, each stage of parenthood had brought its own set of hurdles. Yet, through it all, their love had been the rock solid foundation that had seen them through it all. They had learned to lean on each other, to communicate openly, and to find strength in their partnership.

Thinking back to those early days, when they had struggled just to make ends meet, Seraphina marveled at how far they had come. There had been times when the weight of financial strain felt unbearable, moments when they had to make tough decisions about what to prioritize. Yet, even in those difficult times, Richard's unwavering support and determination had inspired her. They had found joy in the little things cooking together, taking walks, and dreaming about brighter days ahead.

They had faced health scares, too, moments that had tested their resilience. There was that one time when Richard had fallen ill, and the fear that gripped Seraphina had been almost paralyzing. She remembered pacing the hospital corridors, praying for his recovery, clutching their children close to her heart. The experience had brought them even closer, reinforcing the importance of cherishing each moment together.

Countless obstacles had crossed their path, but through it all, their love had remained unwavering. It was a constant, a guiding light that had led them through the darkest of times. Seraphina often reflected on how their love had matured, evolving from the passionate spark of their early days into a deep, abiding connection that was both comforting and exhilarating. They had developed a language all their own, filled with inside jokes and shared glances that spoke volumes.

As she thought about the future, Seraphina felt a surge of hope and excitement. Their family was growing, their children were thriving, and the love that bound them together was as strong as ever. Each milestone they celebrated birthdays, graduations, first days of school felt like a testament to their journey together. They had built a life rich with experiences, filled with laughter, adventure, and love.

No matter what challenges lay ahead, Seraphina knew that as long as they had each other, they could weather any storm. The knowledge that they were a team, facing life's ups and downs together, filled her with peace. She often reminded herself that love didn't mean living a life free of difficulties, rather, it meant having the strength to face those challenges with someone by your side.

And so, as she sat there, bathed in the warm glow of the setting sun, Seraphina smiled to herself. The golden light filtered through the leaves of the trees outside, casting playful shadows on the floor. Love truly was the most powerful force in the universe, the one thing that could conquer any obstacle, transcend any test of time. It was the glue that held their family together, the thread that wove their lives into a beautiful tapestry.

As she looked at her family, her heart full to bursting with love and gratitude, Seraphina knew that there was nothing in the world that they couldn't overcome, as long as they had each other. She took a sip of her tea, savoring its warmth as she watched her children chase each other, their laughter ringing like music.

# Chapter Forty

Seraphina, the Earth Angel, used to spend her days spreading love and light throughout the world. Her presence was like a warm embrace, a soothing balm for those in pain. Wherever she went, she left a trail of comfort, hope, and joy. People would seek her out, drawn to her radiant energy, eager to bask in the glow of her kindness. Children and adults alike felt an inexplicable connection to her, she had a gift for making everyone feel seen and valued.

With her gentle touch, Seraphina healed broken hearts and uplifted weary souls. She would sit with those who needed a listening ear, offering words of wisdom that seemed to flow from an endless well of understanding. Her laughter was infectious, and her smile lit up even the darkest corners of despair. It was said that she could sense the unspoken burdens of those around her, and she had an uncanny ability to ease their pain with just a few kind words.

However, as her own family grew, Seraphina found herself torn between her duty to the world and her responsibilities at home. The arrival of her children had filled her life with joy and purpose, yet it also introduced a complexity she had not anticipated. Suddenly, her days were filled with the demands of motherhood, and she struggled to balance her calling as an Earth Angel with the nurturing of her young ones.

With each passing day, Seraphina's children brought joy and laughter into her life. Their innocent smiles and playful giggles filled her heart with warmth, creating a sanctuary of happiness within her home. She cherished every moment spent with them, from the quiet snuggles during bedtime stories to the boisterous laughter during playtime. Each day was a new adventure, and she delighted in watching them grow and explore the world around them.

Yet, a part of her couldn't help but wonder what God had in store for their growing family next. The responsibilities of motherhood sometimes felt overwhelming, and she worried about how to maintain her connection to her larger purpose while being present for her children. The weight of her dual roles tugged at her heart, leaving her feeling as if she were being pulled in two different directions.

As Seraphina's wings fluttered with uncertainty, she sought guidance in the whispers of the wind and the songs of the birds. Nature had always been her sanctuary, a place where she could commune with the divine. She would often find herself wandering through the forest, listening to the rustling leaves and the gentle babbling of streams, hoping to find clarity amidst the chaos of her thoughts.

In her quiet moments of reflection, she prayed for clarity and understanding, hoping to find a balance between her calling as an Earth Angel and her role as a mother. She asked for the wisdom to navigate the challenges ahead, yearning for a sense of purpose that would encompass both her family and her mission to spread love and light.

One night, as she gazed at the stars shimmering in the vast sky, a gentle voice spoke to her soul. It was a voice that resonated deep within her being, soothing her worries and fears. Dear Seraphina, it whispered, your days of spreading love and light are far from over. Your family is a precious gift, and your love for them is a reflection of the divine.

Tears glistened in Seraphina's eyes as she embraced the message that filled her heart with peace. She realized that her purpose was not confined to the boundaries of the world but encompassed the boundless love she shared with her family. Each hug, each word of encouragement, and each moment spent together was a manifestation of her divine calling.

With renewed strength and determination, she embarked on a journey of motherhood, infusing each moment with love, compassion, and grace. She understood that nurturing her children was a sacred duty, one that allowed her to cultivate the very qualities she had once shared with the world. The laughter of her children became a melody that accompanied her daily life, reminding her of the beauty in simplicity.

As Seraphina's children grew, they learned from her example, and the light she radiated touched the lives of those around them. They watched as their mother demonstrated kindness, compassion, and unwavering faith, embodying the principles of love she had always preached. Through her unconditional love and unwavering devotion, Seraphina continued to spread love and light, not just to the world, but to her family as well.

She instilled in her children the values of empathy and understanding, teaching them to recognize the needs of others. They became little Earth Angels in their own right, reaching out to classmates who felt alone, volunteering their time to help those in need, and spreading joy wherever they went. Seraphina's heart swelled with pride as she witnessed their kindness blossom.

Author

Amanda Ventura is a passionate advocate for self help and personal growth, frequently exploring a wide array of topics that resonate with her experiences and insights. As a linguist, she finds joy in immersing herself in diverse cultures and acquiring new languages, which enriches her understanding of the world. This cultural curiosity not only fuels her writing but also informs her perspectives on spiritual wellness and self expression. With two grown daughters, Ventura, embodies the values of empowerment and open communication, encouraging others to embrace their authentic selves. Through her work, she aspires to inspire and uplift those seeking to navigate their own journeys toward fulfillment and self discovery.

# About the Author

Amanda Ventura, a linguist originally from Texas, has a strong enthusiasm for languages, writing, and culture. Her unique personal experiences have the potential to resonate deeply with many, and she aims to share her story to inspire and connect with a global audience. Amanda Ventura aims to make a positive societal impact by sharing her experiences.

Read more at https://www.amazon.com/author/venturaamanda.